McCALL'S
Introduction to
SCANDINAVIAN COOKING

McCALL'S
Introduction to
SCANDI- NAVIAN COOKING

Edited by Linda Wolfe

GALAHAD BOOKS · NEW YORK CITY

Library of Congress Catalog Card Number: 73-92826
ISBN 0-88365-201-3

Published by arrangement with Saturday Review Press,
division of E. P. Dutton & Co., Inc.

Printed in the United States of America

Contents

Illustrations follow pages 26 and 42

Introduction

Not very long ago Scandinavia was of little interest to Americans. But after World War II, when extensive air travel to Europe began, this country experienced a flurry of excitement about all things Scandinavian. It started when Americans in Europe first encountered Scandinavian silverware, pottery, fabrics, and furniture. So brilliant were these articles in design, always making use of fine materials but always emphasizing simplicity, that Americans began furnishing their homes with Scandinavian objects. Our entire concept of interior decoration was greatly influenced by modern Scandinavian designers and craftsmen. Scandinavian design became synonymous with elegant good taste. Interestingly, the very qualities that distinguish Scandinavian crafts are found in the region's cuisine: Scandinavian cooking, while relying on fine ingredients, always stresses simplicity and is always in elegant good taste.

Scandinavia consists of five countries, all of them northerly, cold, and with long seacoasts. They are Sweden, Denmark, Norway, Finland, and Iceland. The first four are part of the European continent; Iceland is to their west in the North Atlantic. The countries differ from one another in many respects. All have different languages. Sweden, the richest of them, has numerous underground resources that have made her the most industrialized of the Scandinavian countries. Denmark's rich and fertile farmland has allowed her to raise livestock and market their products. Norway is mountainous; Finland is heavily forested; and Iceland is barren and treeless.

Yet the countries have certain features in common that have led to the development of a cuisine that is shared among the five. To begin with, their geography and northern climatic conditions are similar. Winters are long and cold, so that there is only a short growing season. As a result, vegetables play only a minor role in Scandinavian cookery. Similarly, except in Denmark, it is difficult to raise sufficient livestock, so meat and poultry are relatively scarce. All the Scandinavian countries, however, are surrounded by seas in which fish are abundant. For this reason, fish and shellfish form the major part of Scandinavia's cuisine.

Not geography alone but history, too, has shaped the culinary tradition. Scandinavians are descended from the brave seafaring vikings, a rugged people who sailed as far as America long before Columbus did. With no farm produce and little meat, the vikings managed to sustain themselves through long icy winters and on treacherous ocean voyages by preserving their fish, smoking it or salting it or pickling it. By virtue of imagination, they created many ways to eat the same foods and so were able to vary their diet.

Today in Scandinavia the same tradition persists. For example, the herring, which we in America think of as being always of the same size and flavor, is prepared in Scandinavia in countless ways. It can be filleted, sliced, or cut into tidbits; marinated, pickled, jellied, fried, stewed, or baked; combined with vinegar, salt, even sugar, pepper, mustard, ginger or horseradish, onion, fresh dill, sour cream, beets, and cucumbers. And each time it tastes different. The same is true of sardines, cod, and mackerel, which are cooked in various ways for a whole new series of flavors. Moreover, when a Scandinavian does cook meat or poultry, she prepares it with the utmost care and imagination, appreciating the value of these scarce foods.

Another thing all the Scandinavians share is a fondness for a unique style of dining—dining by choices, or what we call smorgasbord. This generous buffet of separate dishes is the first thing that comes to most Americans' minds when we think of Scandinavian cuisine. And although there is much more to Scandinavian cooking than smorgasbord, it is no wonder that we think of it so prominently because it is a way of dining that is gracious in its very essence. We dine by decree: the hostess imposes a single whim or two on her guests. The Scandinavian custom seems more hospitable; guests dine by choices.

There is a charming story among the Scandinavians about the origin of smorgasbord. It holds that the tradition began in viking times when distances were great and people could rarely gather together. When they could, on such occasions as weddings, christenings, and funerals, they invariably stayed for days or weeks—to compensate for the time spent in travel. Consequently they would bring food with them to present to their hosts to make the long visits more pleasant. And they would lay their provisions on the hosts' wide table, each guest competing with the next to make the finest offerings. Those from farms brought cheese and greens; those from the sea and lake areas brought fish; those from the forests brought game and mushrooms and fruits. Whether the story is true or whether smorgasbord came about because the long cold winters required that families put by a great store of smoked and storeable foods, it nevertheless suggests what is today the distinctive characteristic of smorgasbord: generosity.

The word *smorgasbord*, which is Swedish, means literally "sandwich board." Each of the Scandinavian languages has a similar word, which refers to the custom of serving a choice of foods so that the diner may sample different tastes rather than simply one or two. Scandinavians eat smorgasbord frequently. It is the most common late-night supper; it is a frequent lunch or dinner, too. Depending on the wealth of a family, and the number of people being fed, a smorgasbord may consist of only five or six choices or it may have as many as fifteen. In restaurants and at parties, there will be dozens of choices and an array so overwhelming that the diner is as happily bewildered as a child who wanders at Christmastime in a department store's toy rooms.

Smorgasbord is not a helter-skelter affair. There are certain dishes which are required and there is a definite order in which they must be eaten. Since many Scandinavian favorites may appear on a smorgasbord table, eating smorgasbord is a good introduction to the range and variety of Scandinavian cooking. If you will imagine yourself attending the smorgasbord in a fine Swedish restaurant, you may be inspired to create your own version for your next party.

Spread out on a large table, in individual serving dishes and always attractively displayed with decorations of feathery dill, flowerlike parsley, or bright lemon wedges, may be as many as sixty different foods. But smorgasbord is not a single-course meal. It is a meal that consists of four courses: first, a herring course; second, a fish course; next, a cold meat and salad course; last, a course of hot foods.

One starts with the herring, which may be presented in as many as twenty different ways—marinated in wine or cream, salted, smoked, pickled or combined with other ingredients—to name a few. After the herring has been eaten, the diner returns to the table, gets a fresh plate, and samples some of the other cold fish. These may include lobster, shrimp, mussels, sardines, crabmeat, eel, mackerel—any of the denizens of the northern seas and lakes. Now again the diner returns to the table, takes a clean plate, and starts in on the cold meats, such as smoked goose, jellied veal, and sliced roast beef, and the salads made of pickled vegetables or tart fruits. At last it is time for the fourth course, the hot food. This course may include meat or fish. There may be, for example, baked anchovies and potatoes, lamb with dill sauce, poultry, perhaps even roast reindeer.

A smorgasbord may include any dish the hostess selects, provided that she follows the order of the four courses. To make your own smorgasbord, study the recipes in this book and select in each category those that most appeal to you. Choose a few herring dishes, perhaps pickled herring or herring and apple salad. Then make a few other cold fish dishes, such as lobster salad or sardine salad with mustard dressing. Next provide some cold meats and vegetables. You might want to try the country pâté, the chicken in aspic, the pickled beets, and the smorgasbord salad. Then choose your hot food from the poultry and meat chapter—one or two dishes will be sufficient for any home smorgasbord.

One of the great virtues of this method of entertaining is that many of the dishes can be prepared in advance. And, of course, not all the dishes for a smorgasbord must be prepared at home. Even in Scandinavia, hostesses shop at delicatessen and appetizer shops. Thus, before planning the menu, you might make a trip to your local gourmet or specialties shop or just check what tinned fish and appetizers are available at your supermarket. You will undoubtedly discover foods that you can serve without any preparation beyond placing them prettily on a serving plate. Then you might choose to prepare, say, only two hot dishes and a seafood salad.

Being very design-conscious, Scandinavians always set their smorgasbord tables exquisitely. They make use of three decorative items on the table that we would do well to copy. First, they always employ candles—not just a stately candelabrum, but many candles, in holders of wrought iron, crystal, or silver—which are placed around the table to provide color and a flickering warmth. Usually, there will be a floral centerpiece, and flowers will be repeated in other parts of the table's setting: as a motif on the plates, twined around napkins, wreathing the candles. And finally, a further decorative touch is always provided by the small brass or china figurines that Scandinavian women collect specifically to enhance their tables.

Besides using candles and flowers and figurines for your smorgasbord party, have sufficient plates so that a fresh one may be taken for each of the four parts of the meal, as well as silverware and napkin changes.

One other thing is essential on the smorgasbord table: bread. As we've seen, the meaning of the Swedish word *smorgasbord* is "sandwich board." In Denmark, the word for smorgasbord is *smorrebrod* which means "bread and butter." The smorgasbord table may have begun with the viking custom of using flat bread as a plate, upon which to eat other foods. In any event, there must be bread on the smorgasbord table, preferably imported dark Scandinavian bread, if you can obtain it; otherwise, the most interesting breads and rolls you can purchase. Bread is an integral part of the meal; it is not ancillary to it.

What should you serve to drink? It is traditional throughout Scandinavia to start the smorgasbord with aquavit, a drink distilled from potatoes or barley and caraway-flavored. Its name means the "water of life," and to the Scandinavians it is indeed a life-giving drink. Cool when it is first sipped, it quickly sends a glowing warmth through the body.

Aquavit should always be served ice cold. It may be chilled in the freezer for several hours or it may be frozen into its own block of ice. To prepare your own iced aquavit, place a bottle of the liquor in a round, straight-sided two-quart plastic container about seven inches high and four or five inches in diameter. Pour water into the container until it comes to the neck of the bottle. Stand the container upright in the freezer, making sure the bottle is in the center of the container, and freeze it over-night. At dinnertime, immerse the plastic container in very hot water until the ice is loosened. Then lift out the ice-coated bottle. Return it to the freezer until ready to serve. Serve the aquavit by holding it in a nap-kin and pouring the liquor into thimble-sized glasses.

With their aquavit the Scandinavians observe a lovely ritual called *skoaling*, or "toasting." Skoaling is more formal, however, than toasting is in our country. At a dinner party the host always skoals first. Holding his glass raised, he engages the eyes of his guests. They respond by looking deeply and trustingly at him, their glasses held toward the region of their hearts. The essence of the ritual is for a look of trust and warmth to be exchanged between host and guest or, later, between one guest and an-other. Only after the eye-exchange is the aquavit drunk. After the first toast, guests are free to skoal one another or their host. As often as some-one raises his glass and eyes to another for a skoal, that person is required to respond. There is only one restriction, and a very sensible one it is too. At any dinner party with more than six guests, the guests are forbidden to skoal their hostess: She may skoal them to her heart's content, but she is not required to respond to a skoal. Scandinavian tradition recognizes that a hostess should not be forced to drink since any dinner party with more than six guests requires clear thinking on the hostess's part.

The Scandinavians do not drink aquavit all night. They begin with it, but they often then switch to another drink that is the perfect companion to all their foods: beer. If you are making a smorgasbord party, be sure to obtain some of the fine Scandinavian beer, such as Tüborg or Carlsberg, to relax your guests and complement and enhance your foods.

Scandinavian cuisine has many tasty elements that do not appear in a smorgasbord. There are the superb and hearty soups, some of them meals in themselves. And there are the famous great open-faced sandwiches. These artfully constructed sandwiches consist of a single slice of bread topped thinly or thickly or even toweringly with slices of meat, bits of lobster or crab, cooked fish, fine salads, caviar, eel, goose pâté, or what you will. Garnished and decorated as carefully as any dinner dish, they are eaten with a knife and fork.

A number of other famous Scandinavian dishes are holiday fare. Roast goose or a big flavorful ham are the favorite Christmas dishes. They are almost always accompanied by glogg, a Christmas punch made with cognac, Bordeaux wine, and port wine, flavored with cloves, cinnamon, sugar, raisins, and almonds and set aflame before serving.

Perhaps the most famous of all Scandinavian specialties is pastry, particularly the world-famous Danish pastry. Curiously the Danes call their pastry *wienerbrod,* which means "Viennese bread." This is not because the Danes are modest, but because the pastry indeed originated in Vienna. Some hundred years ago all the bakers in Copenhagen went on strike, demanding cash wages instead of the traditional payment of room and board. Their employers promptly fired them, importing German and Viennese bakers to replace the Danes. The Viennese bakers folded butter into yeast dough, a technique unknown in Denmark at the time but one which produced delicious sweet rolls. When the strike was over and the Danish bakers returned to work, they began experimenting with the Viennese technique, making such innovations as adding jam and almond fillings to the dough. Thus arose Danish pastry as we know it. Made into an endless variety of shapes and filled with many different tasty ingredients, Danish pastry is flaky and buttery beyond compare.

It is, however, only one of the delicious baking specialties of Scandinavia. Long before the introduction of wienerbrod a hundred years ago, there was already a tradition of fine, painstaking baking throughout Scandinavia. It may have been because the wintry days are so long and dark that Scandinavian housewives have always loved to bake. Indeed the great Swedish novelist Selma Lagerlof writes in her story "The Eclipse" of an aged woman and her friends who, living in the frozen northern forests, gather together whenever there is any pretext of a celebration to partake of fancy cakes and sweet biscuits. In their cold forests it was hard work to make the land yield anything at all; they were often alone and lonely; and "they grew despondent living like that in the shadow of the mountain" unless they could gather for their little parties of cakes and coffee. Lighting the oven, warming the house, and filling it with sweet smells was their way to alleviate the pains of winter.

Perhaps this is the reason that there are so many and diverse cake and cookie and pastry recipes throughout Scandinavia. We have selected a number of the most interesting ones, such as Sweden's saffron-colored St. Lucia buns, Finnish logs, and many other holiday cookies, to serve as an introduction to this great Scandinavian art.

From meal's start, with its parade of interesting appetizers and fish dishes, to meal's end with its fanciful baked desserts, Scandinavian cuisine offers the American housewife a wealth of simple, yet always elegant, specialties.

Salads & Vegetables

Because of the long cold winters and the short summer growing season, Scandinavians were traditionally deprived of vegetables, at least of the fresh green varieties. Thus they came to venerate vegetables which could be stored and used all year long, particularly the potato. Although potatoes had been discovered in the New World in the early sixteenth century, few Europeans had tried them until the eighteenth century, believing them to be poisonous. In Scandinavia, the potato did not become popular until late in the century. At that time there was a famine. Swedes who had been further south in Europe and seen that no one died of eating potatoes brought some back to feed their families. They quickly discovered how nourishing and tasty the new food was, and shortly the potato became a favorite throughout the region. Even today many Scandinavians eat potatoes twice a day, both at lunch and at dinner having as many as four or five at a time. And sometimes a meat or fish dish will be accompanied by potatoes cooked in two different ways, browned and boiled, or browned and French-fried. Perhaps the most delicious Scandinavian potato recipe is crispy browned potatoes.

Green salads are rare in Scandinavia, but their absence is compensated for by fruit salads, such as the winter-fruit salad bowl or smorgasbord salad. Cabbage, cucumbers, and beets—again, vegetables that can be preserved—are also very popular and interestingly prepared.

SALADS

Tart Apple Salad

4 tart apples	2 to 3 teaspoons sugar
¾ cup heavy cream	Paprika
2 tablespoons lemon juice	

1. Pare apples. Shred, on coarse grater, into medium bowl.
2. Pour cream and lemon juice over apples.
3. Sprinkle with sugar (amount depends on tartness of apples); toss lightly.
4. Refrigerate several hours, or until well chilled.
5. Serve, sprinkled with paprika, as salad or as relish for pork or other meats.

Makes 2 cups.

Green Beans and Tomato Salad

1 cup French-style green beans, parboiled	3 tablespoons olive oil
	1½ tablespoons vinegar
2 tomatoes, sliced thinly	2 tablespoons chopped parsley
1 onion, sliced thinly	Salt and pepper

1. Place the green beans and tomato and onion slices in a large salad bowl.
2. Sprinkle with the oil, vinegar, and parsley and season to taste with salt and pepper. Toss the salad and serve.

Makes 4 servings.

Sauerkraut and Potato Salad

4 medium boiled potatoes, diced	½ cup sauerkraut, drained
	4 tablespoons olive oil
1 to 2 boiled beets, diced	1½ tablespoons vinegar
1 medium onion, diced	Salt and pepper

1. Place the potatoes, beets, onion, and sauerkraut in a large salad bowl.

2. Sprinkle with oil and vinegar, and season to taste with salt and pepper. Toss and serve.

Makes 4 to 6 servings.

Smorgasbord Salad

1 medium cabbage, finely shredded (6 cups)	½ cup seedless raisins
1 cup coarsely chopped fresh spinach	1 teaspoon salt
	¾ cup mayonnaise
2 carrots, grated	4 radishes, grated
2 unpared red apples, cored and diced	

1. Combine cabbage, spinach, carrots, apples, raisins, and salt in large salad bowl.

2. Refrigerate several hours, or until ready to serve. Then toss with mayonnaise, and sprinkle with radishes.

Makes 8 servings.

Winter-Fruit Salad Bowl

1 cup pitted dried prunes	¼ cup water
1 cup water	4 oranges
1 cup dried apricots	2 grapefruit
⅓ cup cream sherry	2 apples

1. In small saucepan, place prunes in 1 cup water and bring to boiling. Remove from heat; cover, and let stand at room temperature 1 hour. Then refrigerate until well chilled.

2. In small saucepan, heat apricots, sherry, and ¼ cup water just until bubbling. Remove from heat; let stand at room temperature 1 hour.

3. Peel oranges and grapefruit, removing white membrane. With sharp knife, cut sections into a large bowl, holding fruit over bowl to catch juice.

4. Wash, quarter, core apples. Do not pare. Cut into ½-inch pieces.

5. Add to orange and grapefruit sections with apricots and their liquid. Toss to mix well. Refrigerate, covered, at least 2 hours.

6. Just before serving, drain prunes, discarding liquid. Arrange all fruits in attractive serving bowl.

Makes 18 servings.

VEGETABLES

Swedish-style Brown Beans

2 cups dried Swedish	¾ cup cider vinegar
brown beans	¾ cup dark corn syrup
6 quarts water	¼ cup light brown sugar,
2 teaspoons salt	firmly packed

1. Wash beans; turn into 3-quart saucepan with water. Refrigerate, covered, overnight.

2. Next day, bring to boiling. Reduce heat; simmer, covered, 1 hour.

3. Add remaining ingredients; simmer, covered, about 4 hours, or until beans are tender and mixture is thick; stir occasionally.

Makes 6 to 8 servings.

Pickled Beets

2 cans (1-pound size)	3 whole cloves
whole beets	4 whole black peppercorns
1 cup white-wine vinegar	1 small bay leaf
½ cup sugar	2 medium onions, peeled
1 teaspoon salt	and thinly sliced

1. Drain beets, reserving 1¼ cups liquid. Place beets in 1½- to 2-quart jar.

2. In medium saucepan, combine vinegar, sugar, salt, cloves, peppercorns, bay leaf, and reserved liquid; bring to boiling. Reduce heat, and simmer, uncovered, 5 minutes.

3. Add onion slices to jar. Pour hot liquid over beets and onions. Refrigerate, covered, several hours.

Makes 6 cups.

Scandinavian Cabbage

2 quarts coarsely shredded	1 teaspoon caraway seed
green cabbage (2 pounds)	1½ teaspoons salt
3 cups boiling water	¼ teaspoon pepper
1 cup commercial sour cream	

1. Cook cabbage in boiling water, covered, 6 to 8 minutes, or until tender but still slightly crisp. Drain very well.

2. In top of double boiler, toss cabbage with rest of ingredients. Cook, covered, over boiling water 15 minutes (cabbage will still be slightly crisp).

Makes 6 servings.

Fried Cucumbers

1½ pounds cucumbers	1 teaspoon prepared
2 eggs	horseradish
2 teaspoons salt	½ cup dry bread crumbs
¼ teaspoon pepper	½ cup butter or margarine

1. Pare cucumbers; slice ¼ inch thick.

2. Beat eggs with salt, pepper, and horseradish in small bowl. Dip cucumber slices in egg mixture, then in crumbs, coating well.

3. Heat butter in large skillet. Fry slices, a few at a time, until golden on both sides. Drain on paper towels; keep warm.

Makes 6 servings.

Pickled Cucumbers

4 large cucumbers	¼ cup sugar
(2½ pounds)	½ teaspoon white pepper
2 tablespoons salt	2 tablespoons snipped fresh
1 cup white vinegar	dill or parsley

1. Scrub cucumbers with vegetable brush; wipe dry with paper towels. Do not pare. Cut cucumbers into thin slices.

2. In medium bowl, lightly toss cucumber with salt. Cover with a plate weighed down with a heavy can. Let stand at room temperature 2 hours.

3. Drain cucumber well; pat dry with paper towels. Place in medium bowl.

4. In small bowl, combine vinegar, sugar, and pepper; mix well. Pour over cucumber slices. Refrigerate, covered, until well chilled—at least 4 hours, or overnight.

5. To serve: Drain cucumber slices well. Turn into serving dish. Sprinkle with dill.

Makes 6 cups.

Crispy Browned Potatoes

6 to 8 potatoes (3 pounds)　　　½ cup dry bread crumbs
½ cup butter or margarine　　　1 teaspoon sugar
2 teaspoons salt

1. Cook unpeeled potatoes in a covered pot in a small amount of boiling, salted water, to cover, for 25 to 30 minutes, or just until tender. Drain; cool slightly. Peel and halve.

2. Preheat oven to 375°F. Melt butter in skillet. Stir in salt, bread crumbs, and sugar. Roll potato halves, a few at a time, in crumb mixture, coating well.

3. Arrange in 11-by-7-by-1½-inch ungreased baking dish; bake 15 to 20 minutes, or until coating is crisp.

Makes 6 to 8 servings.

Horseradish Potatoes

6 potatoes　　　　　　　　　　1 teaspoon salt
2 tablespoons butter　　　　　⅛ teaspoon pepper
2 tablespoons flour　　　　　　1 tablespoon prepared
2 cups milk　　　　　　　　　　　horseradish

1. Preheat oven to 350°F. Peel the potatoes, cut them into shoestrings, and place them in a lightly greased 9-inch baking dish.

2. Prepare the sauce by melting the butter, adding the flour, and gradually stirring in the milk. When sauce is smooth and slightly thickened, add salt and pepper and horseradish and pour the sauce over the potatoes.

3. Bake 45 minutes, or until potatoes are done.

Makes 6 servings.

Lemony Potatoes

4 cups potatoes, peeled　　　2 tablespoons butter
　　　and cubed　　　　　　　4 tablespoons lemon juice
Salt　　　　　　　　　　　　　1 tablespoon chopped parsley

1. Boil the potatoes in salted water for 10 minutes, or until tender.

2. Remove from heat, drain, and place in serving bowl. Add the butter and lemon juice, shaking the bowl gently to let the potato cubes absorb flavor. Sprinkle with parsley and serve.

Makes 6 servings.

Soups & Sandwiches

Throughout Scandinavia, **both soups and** sandwiches are favorite one-course meals. In a cold climate nothing is as welcome as a warming soup. The hearty, meal-in-themselves soups are usually made from the kinds of vegetables that keep for a long time, such as potatoes or cabbage. The Scandinavians are particularly famous for the soups they make of dried and fresh fruits. Fruit soups are eaten warm or cold and are often served as the dessert course, especially during the summer months.

The open-faced sandwich is a regional specialty—no people understand the sandwich as well as the Scandinavians do. To begin with, they admire and create many interesting kinds of bread. The Scandinavians prefer a tightly textured dark sour rye, sliced thin so that the topping's flavor will dominate. The bread is buttered thinly and evenly so that the butter acts as a seal, preventing moist foods from making the bread soggy. Almost anything may be served on top of a Scandinavian sandwich, from pickled herring to roast beef with potato salad. Indeed, there are so many possible combinations that in one Copenhagen restaurant the sandwich menu is four feet and 178 entries long.

SOUPS

Scandinavian Fruit Soup

1 cup pitted dried prunes	¼ cup sugar
1 cup dried apricots	3 tablespoons quick-
¼ cup light or dark raisins	cooking tapioca
½ lemon, sliced	6 cups water
3 (4-inch long) cinnamon	1 cup pared, cubed apple
sticks	

1. Combine all ingredients, except apple cubes, in 3-quart saucepan. Add water; bring to boiling, stirring. Reduce heat; simmer, covered, 20 minutes, or until fruit is tender and tapioca is cooked. Stir occasionally.
2. Add apple cubes; simmer, covered, 5 minutes; remove cinnamon.
3. Serve warm or cold.
Makes 8 servings.

Barley and Mushroom Soup

½ cup pearl barley	½ cup chopped mushrooms
3½ pints stock or water	4 tablespoons butter or margarine
1 onion, finely chopped	1 teaspoon salt
3 carrots, diced	½ teaspoon pepper
4 tablespoons chopped celery	4 tablespoons sour cream

1. Simmer the barley in half the liquid for 1 hour. While it is simmering, boil the onion, carrots, celery, and mushrooms in the other half of the liquid until tender.
2. Add the cooked barley mixture, butter, salt, and pepper to the mushrooms and vegetables.
3. Remove from heat and stir in sour cream. Serve hot or cold.
Makes 8 servings.

Cabbage Soup

1 large head cabbage,	1 quart bouillon
cored and shredded	1 teaspoon salt
¼ cup butter or margarine	½ teaspoon pepper
2 tablespoons brown sugar	

1. Brown the cabbage in butter, stirring occasionally. When brown, add sugar and cook until sugar dissolves completely, stirring constantly.

2. Add the bouillon, salt, and pepper, and simmer covered for 1 hour. Makes 4 servings.

Cauliflower Soup

1 large head of cauliflower	3 tablespoons cream
3 cups salted boiling water	2 tablespoons butter, melted
2 cups chicken stock	Salt and pepper
2 egg yolks	2 tablespoons chopped parsley

1. Trim and wash the cauliflower, break it into small sections, and simmer it in the salted boiling water for 15 minutes, or until the cauliflower is soft.

2. Beat the cauliflower vigorously with a wire whisk until it is minced finely. Add the stock and bring toward boil.

3. While the soup is heating, beat the egg yolks and dilute them with the cream.

4. Just before the soup reaches boiling point, remove it from the heat and stir in the butter and egg yolks. Season to taste with salt and pepper and garnish with parsley.

Makes 4 to 6 servings.

Leek and Potato Soup

4 leeks, sliced	4 cups boiling salted water
5 medium potatoes, peeled and sliced	2 cups milk
3 tablespoons butter	Salt and pepper

1. Sauté the leeks and potatoes in butter in a deep saucepan until golden.

2. Pour the boiling salted water over them and simmer until potatoes are soft.

3. Add the milk and salt and pepper to taste; stir and heat through. Makes 6 to 8 servings.

Yellow-Split-Pea Soup

1 pound quick-cooking dried yellow split peas, washed	1 bay leaf
	2 pounds pork shoulder, bone in
2 quarts boiling water	1 cup finely chopped onion

1 teaspoon dried
   marjoram leaves
¼ teaspoon dried thyme leaves
¼ teaspoon ground ginger

3 teaspoons salt
¼ teaspoon pepper
½ cup water

1. Combine peas, boiling water, and bay leaf in 4½-quart kettle or Dutch oven; bring to boiling. Reduce heat; simmer, covered, 1 hour; stir occasionally.

2. Add pork, onion, marjoram, thyme, and ginger; bring to boiling. Reduce heat, and gently boil, covered, 1 hour and 15 minutes; stir occasionally. Peas and pork should be tender.

3. Stir in salt, pepper, and ½ cup water. Remove pork. Strain soup through coarse strainer; then pour back into kettle, and gently reheat. Meanwhile, slice pork.

4. Serve bowls of soup, along with pork slices on the side and, if desired, sliced pumpernickel.

Makes 6 servings.

SANDWICHES

Roast Beef and Potato Salad Sandwich

4 slices cold roast beef
2 tablespoons soft butter
   or margarine

2 slices dark bread
4 ounces potato salad
1 tablespoon chopped chives

1. Place two roast beef slices on each slice of evenly buttered bread.

2. Top with your favorite kind of potato salad and sprinkle with chives.
Makes 2 open-faced sandwiches.

Blue Cheese and Cucumber Sandwich

1 cucumber
2 ounces blue cheese
2 ounces cream cheese
2 tablespoons soft butter
   or margarine

2 slices dark bread
Salted chopped almonds

1. Peel cucumber, cut in half widthwise, scoop out seeds and pulp with a small spoon.

2. Mix together blue cheese and cream cheese, and stuff mixture into cucumber. Chill ½ hour.

3. Slice cucumber and place on buttered bread. Top with chopped almonds.

Makes 2 open-faced sandwiches.

Pickled-Herring Sandwich

1 loaf unsliced round pumpernickel bread (6 inches in diameter)	1 cup shredded iceberg lettuce
¼ cup soft butter or margarine	3 hard-cooked eggs, quartered
1 medium red onion, thinly sliced	¼ cup grated radishes
1 bunch watercress	2 tablespoons chopped fresh parsley
4 whole pickled herrings, drained	1 cup sour cream
	Beef-aspic glaze (see below)

1. With sharp knife, trim crust from bottom of bread. Cut 4 slices, each ½ inch thick, from bottom.

2. Place bread slices on wire rack. Spread with butter. Separate onion slices into rings. Arrange large rings over butter; top with watercress.

3. Split herrings lengthwise to form 2 strips. Arrange 2 herring strips to form a circle on watercress bed. Place ¼ cup shredded lettuce in center of each herring circle. Garnish each with 3 egg quarters, grated radish, and chopped parsley.

4. With sour cream in pastry tube, pipe a decorative border around herring.

5. Refrigerate until the sandwiches are well chilled—at least ½ hour.

6. Top with glaze. Refrigerate about 1 hour before serving.

Makes 4 open-faced sandwiches.

Beef-Aspic Glaze

⅓ cup sherry	1 can (10½-ounce size) beef consomme, undiluted
2 cups water	
2 envelopes unflavored gelatin	

1. Add water to the sherry in a medium bowl; mix well. Sprinkle gelatin over surface of mixture; let stand 5 minutes to soften gelatin.

2. Bring beef consomme to boiling; add to gelatin mixture, stirring to dissolve gelatin completely.

3. Refrigerate until consistency of unbeaten egg white—1 to 1½ hours. Remelt aspic if too thick.

4. To glaze: Arrange chilled sandwiches on wire rack set on a metal tray. Spoon semiset aspic over surface of chilled sandwiches. (Reuse any

aspic falling on the tray.) Reglaze sandwiches if a thicker glaze is desired. Refrigerate for at least 1 hour before serving.

Makes 3½ cups glaze—enough to glaze 8 to 10 large sandwiches once.

Toasty Sardine Sandwiches

1 can (7-ounce size) skinless and boneless sardines in oil, drained	1 teaspoon lemon juice
	½ teaspoon Worcestershire sauce
	¼ teaspoon onion salt
¼ cup mayonnaise	Dash Tabasco
3 tablespoons finely chopped celery	8 slices white bread
	¼ cup soft butter or margarine
2 tablespoons finely chopped green pepper	

1. In small bowl, mash sardines with a fork.
2. Add mayonnaise, celery, green pepper, lemon juice, Worcestershire, onion salt, and Tabasco to sardines; mix until well blended.
3. Preheat griddle as manufacturer directs.
4. Spread sardine mixture on 4 bread slices; top with rest of slices.
5. Spread butter on outside sides of sandwiches.
6. Grill sandwiches about 5 minutes, or until nicely browned on underside. Turn; grill about 5 minutes, or until browned on other side.

Makes 4 sandwiches.

Sardine Supper Sandwiches

1 loaf unsliced round pumpernickel (6 inches in diameter)	1 cup shredded iceberg lettuce
	2 cans (3¾-ounce size) sardines in curry sauce
¼ cup soft butter or margarine	Lemon juice
1 medium red onion, peeled and thinly sliced	3 hard-cooked eggs, quartered
	¼ cup grated radishes
1 bunch watercress	1 cup sour cream

1. With sharp knife, trim crust from bottom of pumpernickel. Cut 4 slices, each ½ inch thick, from bottom.
2. Place bread slices on wire rack. Spread with butter. Separate onion slices into rings. Arrange large rings over butter; top with watercress.
3. Place ¼ cup shredded lettuce in center of each sandwich. Arrange sardines, spoke fashion, over lettuce; sprinkle sardines generously with lemon juice.
4. Garnish each sandwich with 3 egg quarters and some grated radish.

5. Mound sour cream in center of sandwiches. Refrigerate sandwiches until well chilled—at least ½ hour.

Makes 4 open-faced sandwiches.

Sandwich Torte

1 round loaf white bread
   (10 inches in diameter)

Creamy Egg Filling
6 hard-cooked eggs
1 cup soft butter or margarine
1 to 2 teaspoons curry
   powder
¼ teaspoon salt

Salmon-Butter Filling
1 cup soft butter or margarine
½ pound smoked salmon,
   finely chopped (1 cup)
1 tablespoon ketchup
Dash cayenne

Garnish
1 cup finely chopped parsley
2 tablespoons soft butter
   or margarine
1 teaspoon dried dill weed
½ teaspoon lemon juice
2 smoked salmon slices
4 stuffed green olives
4 small lettuce cups
1 can (3¾-ounce size)
   sardines, drained
1 pimiento, cut into thin strips

1. Remove top and bottom crusts from bread in thin, horizontal slices. Then cut bread crosswise into 4 slices for torte layers. Keep the bread covered until ready to use.

2. Make creamy egg filling: Mash eggs finely with fork. With electric mixer at low speed, cream butter in small bowl. Beat in eggs, curry powder, and salt until smooth.

3. Make salmon-butter filling: With mixer at low speed, cream butter in small bowl. Beat in salmon, ketchup, and cayenne until smooth.

4. Put torte layers together: Spread first layer with half of salmon filling; top with second layer, spread with 1 cup plus 2 tablespoons egg filling; add third layer, spread with rest of salmon filling. Add last layer; then frost top and sides with rest of egg filling. Sprinkle sides with parsley. Refrigerate until very well chilled—2 hours.

5. Meanwhile, mix butter, dill, and lemon juice; spread on salmon slices. Roll each jelly-roll fashion; wrap in waxed paper, and refrigerate.

6. Before serving, garnish top of torte: Place olives in center. Arrange lettuce cups around edge. Slice each salmon roll into four 1-inch rounds; arrange alternately with sardines, in spoke fashion, on lettuce. Lay pimiento strip across each sardine. Cut torte into wedges.

Makes 4 to 6 large open-faced sandwiches.

Eggs & Seafood

Both eggs and seafood figure prominently among the cold dishes on smorgasbord tables, and they are frequently combined to provide a hot supper dish, as in fish soufflé with lobster sauce or scrambled eggs with herring or with sardines. Denmark produces excellent eggs, and all the Scandinavian countries have fine fish. Herring, cod, and mackerel are abundant in the northern seas, and from the many mountain streams come superb trout and salmon.

Scandinavians are as proud of the freshness and quality of their fish as Americans are of their beef. Frequently they buy their fish live from the large cement tanks in the fish market; the fishmonger there nets whatever fish the purchaser selects. Even when fish is bought already killed and iced, it is carefully selected for its freshness. As a result, Scandinavian fish dishes rarely taste "fishy." Instead, like meat, the fish is firm and delicate. To make the delicious baked fish in wine sauce or the fish fillets with dill taste truly Scandinavian, buy as fresh a fish as possible.

Herring and sardines are immensely popular because they were reliably available throughout the north and could be preserved for winter use. There are hundreds of different ways that Scandinavians prepare herring. For smorgasbord, one Stockholm restaurant serves twenty different cold herring dishes, such as the herring and apple salad or the crock of herring. Herring and sardines are also excellent in hot dishes. For a pleasant surprise, try dishes such as the herring and potato casserole or the sardine rabbit.

EGGS

Fish Soufflé with Lobster Sauce

Soufflé
5 egg whites
5 tablespoons butter or
  margarine
2 tablespoons dry bread
  crumbs
1 pound fillet of flounder
2 cups water
⅓ cup unsifted all-
  purpose flour
2 teaspoons salt
⅛ teaspoon pepper
1½ cups milk
¼ teaspoon cream of tartar
4 egg yolks

Lobster Sauce
2 tablespoons butter or margarine
2 tablespoons flour
¾ cup milk
1 cup light cream
1 cup coarsely chopped
  cooked lobster; or 1 can
  (8-ounce size) lobster,
  drained, cut up
¾ teaspoon salt
Dash cayenne
1 egg yolk, slightly beaten

1. Preheat over to 375°F. Let egg whites warm to room temperature in large bowl of electric mixer. Grease 2-quart soufflé dish or casserole with 1 tablespoon butter. Coat inside with bread crumbs.

2. Place fish flat in large skillet with 2 cups water; bring to boiling. Reduce heat; simmer, covered, 5 minutes, or until fish can be easily flaked with fork.

3. Drain very well, reserving ¼ cup liquid for lobster sauce. Flake fish, and measure 2 cups.

4. Melt rest of butter in medium saucepan. Remove from heat; stir in flour, salt, and pepper until smooth. Then stir in milk; bring mixture to boiling, stirring, over medium heat. Remove from heat; let cool for 10 minutes.

5. With mixer at high speed, beat egg whites with cream of tartar just until stiff peaks form when beater is slowly raised. In small bowl, with mixer at high speed, beat egg yolks until light and fluffy.

6. Stir flaked fish and egg yolks into white sauce until well combined. Turn mixture onto egg whites; with a spatula or rubber scraper, using an under-and-over motion, gently fold into whites until well combined. Turn into soufflé dish.

7. Make top hat: With back of large spoon, make deep path around top of soufflé, 1 inch from edge. Set dish in pan containing about 1 inch hot water; bake 55 minutes.

8. While soufflé bakes, make lobster sauce: Melt butter in small saucepan; remove from heat. Stir in flour until smooth. Then add reserved fish liquid, milk, and cream; bring to boiling, stirring. Remove from heat. Add lobster, salt, cayenne, and egg yolk; cook, stirring, over low heat just until lobster is hot.

9. When soufflé is done, serve it at once with lobster sauce.

Makes 6 servings.

Scrambled Eggs with Herring

1 can (14-ounce size) herring in tomato sauce	⅓ cup thinly sliced green onion
	⅓ cup chopped celery
8 eggs	1 can (3-ounce size) sliced mushrooms, drained, or
¼ cup light cream	¼ pound fresh
⅛ teaspoon celery salt	
⅛ teaspoon pepper	2 tablespoons finely chopped fresh parsley
¼ cup butter or margarine	

1. Remove herring from sauce; discard sauce. Split herring lengthwise; remove bones. Flake herring with fork.

2. In large bowl, with rotary beater, beat eggs, cream, celery salt, and pepper just until combined but not frothy.

3. In 2 tablespoons hot butter in large skillet, sauté onion, celery, and mushrooms, stirring occasionally, until tender—about 5 minutes.

4. In same skillet, heat remaining butter. Add egg mixture; cook over low heat. As eggs start to set at bottom, gently lift cooked portion with spatula, letting uncooked part flow to bottom of pan.

5. When eggs are partially set, stir in herring. Cover skillet; cook 2 minutes. Serve at once, sprinkled with parsley, on heated platter.

Makes 4 to 6 servings.

Scrambled Eggs with Sardines

8 eggs	⅓ cup thinly sliced green onions
¼ cup light cream	1 can (3-ounce size) sliced mushrooms, drained, or
⅛ teaspoon celery salt	¼ pound fresh
⅛ teaspoon pepper	
4 tablespoons butter or margarine	1 can (3¾-ounce size) skinless and boneless sardines in oil, drained
⅓ cup chopped celery	

1. In medium bowl, with rotary beater, beat eggs, cream, celery salt, and pepper just until combined but not frothy.
2. In large skillet, melt 2 tablespoons butter.
3. Add egg mixture to butter; cook over low heat. As eggs start to set at bottom, gently lift cooked portion with spatula, letting uncooked part flow to bottom of pan.
4. Meanwhile, in medium skillet, melt remaining butter. Add celery and onions; sauté 3 minutes.
5. Add mushrooms and sardines to sautéed vegetables; cook, over low heat, until hot—3 to 5 minutes.
6. Spoon eggs onto heated serving platter. Arrange sardines over top; spoon vegetables over.

Makes 4 to 6 servings.

Stuffed Eggs

6 hard-cooked eggs, chilled and shelled	2 teaspoons prepared mustard
½ cup finely chopped smoked salmon (4 ounces)	¼ teaspoon salt
	Dash pepper
¼ cup mayonnaise	6 black pitted olives, drained
1 tablespoon chopped fresh parsley	1 pimiento, drained

1. Halve eggs lengthwise. Remove yolks to a small bowl. Reserve whites.
2. Mash yolks with fork. Add salmon, mayonnaise, parsley, mustard, salt, and pepper; mix well.
3. Fill each white with yolk mixture, mounding it high. Garnish with crescent-shaped pieces of olive and bits of pimiento.
4. Refrigerate, covered, at least 1 hour before serving.
Makes 12.

Deviled Eggs

12 hard-cooked eggs, chilled and shelled	½ teaspoon salt
	Paprika
¾ cup mayonnaise	
1 teaspoon dry mustard	Endive
½ teaspoon dill	Assorted cold cuts

1. Halve eggs lengthwise. Remove yolks, being careful not to break

whites. Place yolks in small bowl. Add mayonnaise, mustard, dill, and salt; beat with electric mixer until smooth.

2. Place yolk mixture in pastry bag with star tip; press out into egg-white halves, filling generously. Sprinkle with paprika.

3. Refrigerate, covered, until well chilled—several hours.

4. To serve: Arrange on endive-lined platter with cold cuts.

Makes 24.

Sardine Deviled Eggs

6 hard-cooked eggs, chilled and shelled	1 teaspoon Worcestershire sauce
1 can (3¾-ounce size) sardines in mustard sauce, undrained	¼ teaspoon salt
	Dash cayenne
2 tablespoons mayonnaise	1 tablespoon chopped fresh parsley
1 tablespoon pickle relish, drained	

1. Halve eggs lengthwise. Remove the yolks, and set the whites aside.

2. In medium bowl, combine sardines and yolks. With fork, mash till smooth. Add remaining ingredients, except parsley; mix well.

3. Fill each egg white with yolk mixture, mounding high.

4. Top with parsley, and refrigerate until well chilled.

Makes 12.

SEAFOOD

Baked Fish in White Wine

1½ cups very thinly sliced carrots	½ cup thinly sliced celery and leaves
Boiling water	2 teaspoons salt
1½ cups finely chopped onion	⅛ teaspoon pepper
¼ pound fresh mushrooms, sliced; or 1 can (3-ounce size) mushroom caps, drained	1 slice halibut or cod (2 pounds)
	6 thin lemon slices
3 tablespoons chopped fresh parsley	3 bacon slices, chopped
	¾ cup dry white wine or chicken broth

1. Preheat oven to 375°F. In small saucepan, cover carrots with boiling water; bring to boiling. Boil, covered, 5 minutes. Drain.

2. Arrange carrots, onion, mushrooms, parsley, and celery in bottom of large, shallow bake-and-serve pan. Sprinkle with 1 teaspoon salt and ⅛ teaspoon pepper.

3. Place fish on vegetables; sprinkle with rest of salt. Overlap lemon slices across fish. Sprinkle with bacon. Pour on white wine. Cover top of the pan completely with foil; then bake 20 minutes.

4. Remove foil; bake 15 to 20 minutes longer, or until fish can be easily flaked with fork. Serve right from pan.

Makes 6 servings.

Fish Fillets with Dill

8 fish fillets	½ cup minced fresh parsley
1 teaspoon salt	½ cup minced fresh dill
½ teaspoon pepper	¼ cup boiling water

1. Preheat oven to 350°F. Sprinkle fish with salt and pepper.

2. Butter a shallow baking dish and sprinkle with half the parsley and dill. Place the fish on top of this bed; then add the remaining parsley and dill.

3. Pour boiling water into baking dish and bake fish 20 minutes, or until it flakes easily when lifted with a fork.

Makes 6 to 8 servings.

Herring-and-Potato Casserole

3 cups cooked, sliced potatoes	1 jar (12-ounce size) herring tidbits in wine sauce, drained
5 tablespoons butter or margarine	Pepper
1¼ cups coarsely chopped onion	¾ cup light cream
	½ cup dry bread cubes (¼-inch size)

1. Preheat oven to 350°F. Lightly grease a 1½-quart casserole.

2. In 2 tablespoons hot butter in small skillet, sauté onion until golden —about 5 minutes.

3. In prepared casserole, layer one-third potatoes, half of herring, and half of onion. Sprinkle lightly with pepper; dot with 1 tablespoon butter. Repeat; then top with remaining potatoes. Then pour on cream.

4. Melt remaining 1 tablespoon butter; toss with bread cubes. Sprinkle bread cubes over potatoes. Bake, uncovered, 20 minutes, or until heated through.

Makes 4 servings.

Herring in Sour Cream

3 matjes-herring fillets	2 bay leaves
1 medium onion	¾ cup sour cream
24 whole black peppercorns	¼ cup sauterne

1. Rinse fillets in cold water; drain; dry on paper towels. Cut crosswise into 1-inch pieces. Then slice onion into thin rings.

2. In medium bowl, layer onion rings, black peppercorns, bay leaves, and herring pieces.

3. Combine sour cream and wine. Pour over herring mixture, mixing gently to combine.

4. Refrigerate, covered, 8 hours, or overnight.

Makes 2 cups.

Note: Herring in sour cream may be stored, covered, in refrigerator for 3 days.

Herring Salad

1 can (1-pound size) sliced pickled beets	¼ cup mayonnaise
	2 tablespoons sugar
1 jar (12-ounce size) herring in wine sauce	Dash white pepper
	2 tablespoons water
1½ cups diced cooked potato	
½ cup diced pared apple	2 hard-cooked eggs, cut
⅓ cup diced dill pickle	into wedges
¼ cup finely chopped onion	Parsley sprigs

1. Drain beets, reserving ¼ cup liquid; dice. Drain herring; dice.

2. In large bowl, combine beets, herring, potato, apple, pickle, and onion.

3. In small bowl, combine reserved beet liquid, the mayonnaise, sugar, pepper, and 2 tablespoons water; mix well. Add to beet mixture, mixing until well blended.

4. Rinse a 6-cup mold with cold water. Fill with salad, pressing into mold firmly.

5. Refrigerate, covered, until well chilled—several hours.
6. To serve: Unmold on serving platter. Garnish with hard-cooked eggs and parsley sprigs and serve with dark pumpernickel.
Makes 8 servings.

Herring-Apple Salad

3 matjes-herring fillets
1 medium onion, sliced
½ cup sliced celery
1 apple, peeled and sliced
½ cup pecan halves
1 teaspoon lemon juice

⅛ teaspoon pepper
1 tablespoon dry bread crumbs

Crisp lettuce leaves
2 tablespoons chopped parsley

1. Rinse herring, and dry well on paper towels. Cut crosswise into 1-inch pieces.
2. Chop herring with onion, celery, apple, and pecans into small pieces.
3. Add lemon juice, pepper, and bread crumbs to herring mixture; continue to chop until well blended.
4. Line a small serving platter with lettuce leaves. Mound herring mixture in center of platter; sprinkle with parsley.
Makes 4 to 6 servings.

Crock of Herring

1 medium carrot, pared
1 medium onion, peeled
3 jars (12-ounce size)
   herring in wine sauce,
   undrained

12 pitted black olives
¼ teaspoon whole black
   peppercorns

1. Cut carrot on diagonal into ⅛-inch-thick slices. Slice onion paper-thin.
2. In large glass container or bowl, combine carrot and onion slices, herring in wine sauce, black olives, and whole peppercorns.
3. Refrigerate at least 24 hours.
Makes 12 servings.

Pickled Herring

1 whole Iceland salt herring,
   head and tail removed, or
1 can (6-ounce size)
   schmaltz-herring fillets

¾ cup sugar
½ teaspoon whole allspice,
   crushed
1 medium red onion, sliced

4 to 6 sprigs fresh dill,	1 cup water
tied with twine	1 cup Swedish or white vinegar
1 bay leaf	

1. Rinse herring well. In medium bowl, add cold water to herring to cover. Refrigerate, covered, 24 hours, changing water once. Next day, remove herring from water; dry on paper towels.

2. To fillet herring: Starting from tail end of herring, loosen and peel off skin with sharp paring knife. With head end of herring at right, split herring in half lengthwise, cutting just above center bone. Remove upper half. Carefully cut lower half of herring away from bone. Lift out bones, and discard. You will have 2 fillets.

3. Cut each fillet crosswise into 1-inch pieces.

4. Meanwhile, in medium saucepan, combine sugar, allspice, onion, dill, bay leaf, and water. Cook, over medium heat, stirring constantly, until sugar dissolves; bring to boiling. Reduce heat; simmer, uncovered, 5 minutes.

5. With slotted utensil, remove and reserve onion rings; remove and discard dill. Stir in vinegar. Let mixture cool completely.

6. In pint jar with tight-fitting lid, layer herring alternately with onion. Fill jar to top with cooled vinegar mixture; cover. Refrigerate at least 24 hours before using. (Herring may be stored in refrigerator for a week.)

Makes 4 servings.

Herring Salad Platter

	Sauce
1 jar (12-ounce size) herring tidbits in wine sauce	¾ cup sour cream
4 hard-cooked eggs, sliced	2 tablespoons ketchup
½ bunch parsley or dill	1 tablespoon prepared horseradish
4 medium-sized ripe tomatoes	⅛ teaspoon celery salt
	Dash cayenne

1. Drain herring, reserving 1 teaspoon liquid for sauce.

2. Mound herring in center of round serving platter. Arrange egg slices, overlapping them, around the herring.

3. Surround eggs with parsley. Cut each tomato into 8 wedges; arrange tomatoes on parsley. Refrigerate at least 1 hour.

4. Just before serving, make sauce: In medium bowl, with rotary beater, beat sour cream until light. With rubber scraper, fold in reserved herring liquid and rest of sauce ingredients. Pass sauce with salad.

Makes 4 to 6 servings.

Lobster Salad

6 (8-ounce size) frozen
   rock-lobster tails
1 tablespoon salt
4 lemon slices
1 bay leaf
2 celery stalks, cut up
¼ pound small mushrooms
⅓ cup lemon juice
4 hard-cooked eggs

Marinated Vegetables
2 cans (15-ounce size) white
   asparagus spears, drained
1 can (15-ounce size)
   whole tiny carrots, drained

1 cup bottled oil-and-
   vinegar salad dressing

Dressing
1½ cups mayonnaise
2 cups sliced celery
¼ cup chopped green pepper
1 teaspoon salt
½ teaspoon paprika
Dash cayenne

Crisp salad greens
1 drained pimiento,
   cut into 2-inch strips

1. In large kettle, bring 3 quarts water to boiling. Add frozen lobster tails, salt, the lemon slices, bay leaf, and cut-up celery; return to boiling. Reduce heat, and simmer, covered, 15 minutes. Drain, and cool.

2. Remove meat from lobster tails in one piece, being careful to keep 3 shells intact for garnish. Cut lobster meat into bite-sized pieces—about 1 inch. Refrigerate, covered, until chilled—at least 2 hours.

3. Meanwhile, slice mushrooms right through stems; toss with lemon juice. Refrigerate, covered.

4. Shell eggs; chop coarsely. Refrigerate, covered.

5. Prepare marinated vegetables: Arrange asparagus and carrots in shallow dish. Pour oil-and-vinegar dressing over all. Refrigerate, covered, at least 1 hour.

6. Make dressing: In large mixing bowl, combine mayonnaise with sliced celery, green pepper, salt, paprika, and cayenne; mix well. Refrigerate, covered.

7. Add chilled lobster meat, sliced mushrooms, and chopped eggs to dressing; toss lightly until well combined. Refrigerate until very well chilled—several hours.

8. To serve: Mound lobster salad on salad greens in center of serving platter. With slotted utensil, lift marinated vegetables out of oil-and-vinegar dressing, and arrange around edge of platter. Decorate asparagus spears with pimiento strips. Garnish salad with lobster shells.

Makes 8 to 10 servings.

Sardine Savories

Filling
1 can (8-ounce size) sardines
   in tomato sauce, drained
2 crisp-cooked bacon
   slices, crumbled
2 tablespoons mayonnaise
¼ cup finely chopped celery
1 tablespoon lemon juice

1 tablespoon onion, minced

1 package (8-ounce size)
   refrigerator crescent rolls
4 teaspoons butter or margarine,
   melted
1 egg yolk
1 tablespoon water

1. Preheat oven to 400°F.

2. Make filling: In small bowl, using fork, mash sardines. Add remaining filling ingredients; mix well.

3. Separate rolls. On lightly floured surface, roll two rolls, placed side by side, into an 8-inch square. Brush with 1 teaspoon butter. Cut into 8 (4-by-2-inch) rectangles. Repeat with rest of rolls to make 32 rectangles.

4. On half of each rectangle, place 1 rounded teaspoon filling. Fold other half over filling to make a 2-inch square. Press edges to seal; slit top.

5. Place, 2 inches apart, on ungreased cookie sheet. Brush with egg yolk beaten with water.

6. Bake 10 to 12 minutes, or until deep golden brown. Serve hot. Makes 32.

Hot Sardine Potato Salad

2 pounds medium potatoes
8 raw bacon slices, diced
1 cup thinly sliced celery
½ cup sliced onion
2 tablespoons flour
3 tablespoons brown sugar
½ teaspoon salt

¼ teaspoon coarsely ground
   black pepper
⅓ cup white vinegar
1⅓ cups water
1 can (6¼-ounce size) sardines
   in oil with spices, drained

1. Cook unpeeled potatoes, covered, in boiling water just until tender—about 30 minutes.

2. Drain potatoes; cool. Peel; cut into slices ⅛ inch thick.

3. Sauté bacon in skillet, over low heat, until crisp; remove from heat. Remove bacon; add to potatoes. Reserve 5 tablespoons drippings.

4. In same skillet, in 2 tablespoons reserved drippings, sauté celery and onion until tender but crisp—about 2 minutes. Add to potatoes.

5. Heat remaining reserved drippings. Stir in flour, brown sugar, salt, and pepper until smooth. Gradually add vinegar and water.

6. Bring to boiling; reduce heat, and simmer, stirring, 5 minutes.
7. Add dressing and sardines to potatoes; toss lightly to combine.
Makes 4 to 6 servings.

Sardine Rabbit

2 tablespoons butter	1 teaspoon Worcestershire sauce
1 pound sharp Cheddar	2 cans (3¾-ounce size) skinless
cheese, grated	and boneless sardines in oil,
½ cup milk	drained
1 egg	4 toast slices, halved
½ teaspoon dry mustard	

1. In medium saucepan, melt butter slowly.
2. Add cheese and milk; cook, over low heat and stirring frequently, until cheese melts. Remove from heat.
3. In small bowl, beat egg with mustard and Worcestershire. Gradually add to cheese mixture, stirring until well combined.
4. Stir, over low heat, until mixture is heated through and smooth—about 5 minutes.
5. Arrange sardines on toast slices.
6. Pour sauce over sardines.
Makes 4 servings.

Sardine Salad Platter

1 can (3¾-ounce size)	**Sauce**
smoked sardines	¾ cup mayonnaise
1 can (4⅝-ounce size)	2 tablespoons prepared mustard
boneless sardines in oil	with horseradish or
1 can (3¾-ounce size)	2 tablespoons mustard and
sardines in tomato sauce	1 teaspoon horseradish
4 hard-cooked eggs, sliced	½ teaspoon cider vinegar
½ bunch fresh dill	⅛ teaspoon seasoned salt
2 medium-sized ripe	
tomatoes	

1. Drain sardines. Place in separate mounds in center of large, round serving platter. Arrange egg slices, overlapping, around the sardines.
2. Surround eggs with dill. Cut each tomato into 8 wedges; arrange tomatoes on dill. Refrigerate 1 hour.
3. Just before serving, make sauce: In small bowl, combine all sauce

ingredients until thoroughly blended. Pass sauce with salad. Serve with buttered rye bread.

Makes 4 to 6 servings.

Sardine Salad with Mustard Dressing

Dressing
1 egg, slightly beaten
¼ cup vinegar
1 tablespoon butter or
   margarine
1 tablespoon sugar
2 tablespoons prepared
   mustard
½ teaspoon paprika

3 cans (3¾-ounce size) skinless
   and boneless sardines in oil,
   drained
1 cup sliced black olives
½ cup sliced celery
¼ cup sliced green onions
½ cup sour cream

Lettuce leaves

1. In small saucepan, combine egg, vinegar, butter, sugar, mustard, and paprika; cook, stirring and over low heat, until slightly thickened— about 5 minutes. Cool.

2. In large bowl, combine sardines, olives, celery, onions, sour cream, and dressing. Toss until combined.

3. Refrigerate at least 2 hours.

4. Serve on lettuce.

Makes 6 servings.

Shrimp Salad

4 jars (2¾-ounce size)
   tiny shrimp (about 3 cups)
1 cup mayonnaise
1 tablespoon lemon juice
½ cup diced,
   pared cucumber

½ cup diced tomato, without
   seeds and excess juice
½ cup cooked peas

Boston- or iceberg-lettuce
   leaves, crisped, chilled
Lemon slices

1. Drain shrimp, reserving some of the largest for garnish.

2. In large bowl, combine mayonnaise, lemon juice, cucumber, tomato, peas, and shrimp.

3. Refrigerate, covered, until well chilled—several hours.

4. To serve: Line salad bowl with lettuce leaves. Arrange shrimp mixture on lettuce. Garnish top with rows of shrimp and lemon slices.

Makes 3 cups.

Meat & Poultry

The Scandinavians treat meat and poultry with great care and concern because only in recent years has there been an ample supply of them. Many Scandinavian meat recipes are designed to stretch the precious ingredient, as in the famous Swedish meatballs where gingersnaps make the meat tasty yet economical. Danish meatballs, although less well known, are also good.

Like the Russians, who found that fruits make a good companion to meats when vegetables are scarce, the Scandinavians excel at meat and fruit combinations. Boiled tongue with prunes, veal with prune stuffing, and ham made with apple cider all rely on fruit flavors to enhance the meat—and you will find these combinations work beautifully.

Poultry, although eaten rarely, is admirably prepared. A favorite Scandinavian recipe is chicken in aspic. The traditional and beloved Christmas dish is roast goose with apple and prune stuffing.

MEAT

Country Pâté

1 pound calf's liver
¾ pound ground pork fat
¼ pound ground veal

3 tablespoons butter or
    margarine
¾ cup chopped onion

5 tablespoons flour
1⅓ cups milk
3 eggs
2 tablespoons brandy
2 teaspoons salt
¾ teaspoon pepper

¼ teaspoon ground allspice
¼ teaspoon ground mace
6 slices uncooked bacon
1 can (3-ounce size) whole
   mushrooms, drained, or
¼ pound fresh

1. Rinse liver; pat dry with paper towels. Cut into small pieces. Put through food grinder twice, using finest blade. Or put liver, one third at a time, in electric blender, and blend at high speed until smooth. Turn into large bowl; stir in pork fat and veal.

2. Preheat oven to 350°F. Grease a 5- or 6-cup casserole.

3. In hot butter in medium saucepan, sauté onion until tender—about 5 minutes. Stir in flour until well combined. Gradually stir in milk; bring to boiling, stirring constantly. Reduce heat, and simmer 1 minute.

4. Add to liver mixture, along with eggs, brandy, salt, pepper, allspice, and mace; stir until well blended. Turn into prepared casserole.

5. Place in roasting pan; pour hot water to 2-inch level around casserole.

6. Bake, uncovered, 1 hour and 45 minutes. Let cool at least 1 hour before serving.

7. Just before serving, in large skillet, fry bacon until crisp. Drain on paper towels. Pour off all but 2 tablespoons drippings.

8. In hot bacon drippings, sauté mushrooms until golden. Arrange with bacon over pâté. Serve warm, with bread and sweet butter and pickled beets, if desired.

Makes 30 buffet servings.

Note: Pâté can be made ahead of time and served cold or warmed up. Garnish just before serving.

Scandinavian Stuffed Cabbage

1 leafy green cabbage
   (5½ pounds)
4 quarts boiling water
1 quart ice water
3 tablespoons butter or
   margarine
⅓ cup finely
   chopped onion
6 teaspoons finely
   chopped fresh parsley
¾ pound ground chuck

¼ pound ground pork
⅓ cup cooked white rice
1 egg, slightly beaten
1 teaspoon Worcestershire sauce
1 teaspoon salt
⅛ teaspoon pepper
¼ teaspoon ground allspice
1½ cups boiling water
1 uncooked bacon slice
2 cans (10½-ounce size)
   beef consommé, undiluted

1 tablespoon dark corn syrup	Few drops bottled gravy
2 tablespoons flour	seasoning

1. Wash cabbage in cold, running water. In deep saucepan, cover cabbage with boiling water; boil, with lid on, 5 minutes. Remove cabbage. With sharp knife, remove 6 loose outer leaves. Plunge these into ice water; set aside for garnishing finished dish.

2. Return rest of cabbage to boiling water. Cover; boil 20 minutes. Drain.

3. Meanwhile, prepare meat filling: In 1 tablespoon butter in small skillet, sauté onion and 5 teaspoons parsley. In medium bowl, combine sautéed vegetables, meats, rice, egg, Worcestershire sauce, salt, pepper, allspice, and ½ cup boiling water; toss with fork.

4. With sharp knife, trim base of cabbage core so cabbage will stand level. Carefully fold back 4 top leaves. Cut 5-inch circle in center of cabbage top.

5. With serrated grapefruit knife, remove and discard cabbage from circled area, leaving cavity about 2½ inches deep. Shell should be 1 inch thick.

6. Fill cavity lightly with meat mixture, mounding slightly in center. Crush 12-inch square of foil over meat; fold 4 outer leaves around foil. Place folded bacon slice under cabbage base; secure with string.

7. In deep saucepan, combine consomme, corn syrup, and 1 cup boiling water. Place cabbage, base down, in liquid. Cover; simmer 60 to 75 minutes, or until fork-tender. Remove to hot serving platter. Fold back outer leaves, and remove foil. Keep cabbage warm. Reserve cooking liquid.

8. Make sauce: Melt remaining butter in small saucepan; remove from heat. Smoothly stir in flour, then 1¾ cups reserved cooking liquid and the gravy seasoning. Bring to boiling, stirring, until thickened.

9. Brush meat with a little sauce, and sprinkle with remaining parsley. Dip reserved cabbage leaves into hot sauce; drain. Fold around cabbage; secure with wooden picks, if necessary.

10. To serve, cut cabbage in wedges. Pass sauce in gravy boat.

Makes 6 servings.

Swedish Meatballs

20 (2-inch size)	½ cup milk
gingersnaps	1 egg, slightly beaten

1 pound ground chuck
½ pound lean ground pork
¼ cup finely
   chopped onion
1 teaspoon salt
½ teaspoon pepper
¼ teaspoon ground allspice
¼ cup butter or margarine

¼ cup unsifted all-
   purpose flour
1½ cups water
2 beef-bouillon cubes,
   crumbled

Parsley sprigs

1. With rolling pin, crush gingersnaps between 2 sheets of waxed paper. Measure 1¼ cups.

2. In large bowl, combine gingersnap crumbs with milk and egg. Add chuck, pork, onion, salt, pepper, and allspice. Using hands, mix well to combine.

3. Refrigerate, covered, 1 hour.

4. With moistened hands, shape mixture into meatballs, 1½ inches in diameter.

5. Preheat oven to 325°F.

6. In hot butter in large skillet, sauté meatballs (just enough at one time to cover bottom of skillet) until browned all over. Remove to a 2-quart casserole as they brown.

7. Remove the skillet from heat. Pour off drippings, reserving ¼ cup, adding more butter if necessary.

8. Stir flour smoothly into drippings. Gradually stir in 1½ cups water. Add bouillon cubes.

9. Bring mixture to boiling, stirring constantly. Strain over meatballs.

10. Bake, covered, 1 hour. Garnish with parsley sprigs. Serve with noodles, if desired.

Makes 6 servings.

Danish Meatballs

Meatballs
1 pound ground chuck
1 pound ground pork
1 cup finely chopped
   onion
½ cup finely chopped
   parsley
½ cup dry bread crumbs
2 teaspoons salt

½ teaspoon ground
   allspice
¼ teaspoon pepper
1 cup milk
1 egg

2 tablespoons flour
¼ cup butter or margarine

Sauce
2 tablespoons flour
1½ cups water
1 beef-bouillon cube

Dash pepper

Chopped parsley

1. Make meatballs: In large bowl, combine all meatball ingredients, except flour and butter. Mix well with hands to combine.

2. Refrigerate, covered, 1 hour.

3. With moistened hands, shape mixture into balls, 2 inches in diameter.

4. Roll the meatballs lightly in 2 tablespoons flour, coating them completely.

5. In hot butter in 10-inch skillet, brown meatballs well (just enough at one time to cover bottom of skillet). Remove from skillet as they brown.

6. Make sauce: Remove skillet from heat. Pour off drippings, reserving 2 tablespoons.

7. Stir 2 tablespoons flour smoothly into drippings. Gradually add 1½ cups water, bouillon cube, and pepper; bring to boiling, stirring.

8. Add meatballs; simmer, covered, 15 minutes.

9. Turn meatballs and sauce into serving dish; sprinkle with parsley. Serve with sweet-and-sour red cabbage and browned potatoes, if desired. Makes 6 to 8 servings.

Boiled Tongue with Prunes

1 (4- to 5-pound size)
  smoked beef tongue
1 can (1-pound, 12-ounce
  size) whole tomatoes,
  undrained

3 tablespoons brown sugar
2 tablespoons lemon juice
½ teaspoon salt
⅛ teaspoon pepper
2 cups large pitted dried prunes

1. In large kettle, cover tongue with cold water.

2. Bring to boiling. Then reduce heat, and simmer, covered, for 2 hours.

3. Drain tongue; let cool slightly. At thick end, trim off fat and gristle. Remove skin: With tip of knife, slit skin on underside from thick end to tip. Loosen skin at thick end; carefully peel off, and discard. Remove and discard root.

4. In same kettle, combine tomatoes, sugar, lemon juice, salt, and pepper; bring to boiling, stirring to break up tomatoes. Simmer, uncovered, 5 minutes.

5. Add tongue and prunes; simmer, covered, 1½ hours, or until tongue is tender. Turn tongue in liquid every 30 minutes.

6. Remove tongue to warm serving platter. Remove prunes and tomatoes from kettle; arrange around tongue.
Makes 6 to 8 servings.

Glazed Smoked Tongue

2 (3½- to 4-pound size)	1 envelope unflavored gelatin
smoked beef tongues	2 hard-cooked eggs
2 large onions,	Black olives
peeled and quartered	Pimiento, drained
10 whole black peppercorns	Green-pepper strips
2 whole cloves	
2 bay leaves	Ice tray (see p. 40)
½ teaspoon mustard seed	Parsley sprigs
4 quarts water	Prepared mustard

1. Wash tongues. Place in large kettle with onions, peppercorns, cloves, bay leaves, mustard seed, and about 4 quarts water, or enough to cover.

2. Bring to boiling; reduce heat, and simmer, covered, 2½ to 3 hours, or until tongues are tender.

3. Lift tongues out of stock, and plunge into cold water. Strain enough stock to make 1 cup, and refrigerate; discard rest of stock.

4. Remove skin from tongues: With sharp knife, gently slit skin on underside from thick end to tip. Peel off skin, and remove and discard root. Refrigerate tongues until chilled—at least 2 hours.

5. To make glaze: In small saucepan, sprinkle gelatin over cold reserved stock; let stand 5 minutes to soften. Cook over low heat, stirring, until gelatin is dissolved.

6. Cool glaze quickly: Set saucepan of stock in bowl of ice cubes; let stand, stirring often, until consistency of unbeaten egg white—10 to 15 minutes.

7. Remove one tongue from refrigerator, and place, root end down, on rack in shallow pan. Pour glaze evenly over tongue, coating well.

8. Cut white part of eggs, the olives, and pimiento into shapes and use with green-pepper strips to decorate glazed tongue. Refrigerate 30 minutes.

9. Place glaze that has collected in pan under the rack in small saucepan; cook over low heat, stirring, just until melted but not hot. Spoon carefully over decorated tongue to cover completely. Refrigerate until firm—at least 2 hours.

10. To serve: Thinly slice plain cooked tongue. Place decorated tongue in center of ice tray. Brush rest of ice tray lightly with salad oil. Then arrange sliced tongue around decorated one. Garnish with parsley. Pass mustard.

Makes 10 to 12 servings.

Ice Tray

1. The day before needed, fill large shallow roasting pan with cold water. Freeze overnight.

2. To remove: Invert into a shallow aluminum pan a little longer than the ice. Place hot, damp towel over bottom of pan, and shake to release ice. Keep frozen until serving time.

3. To keep ice level, push crushed foil underneath block. Arrange food on top, as directed in recipe.

Spiced Veal Roll

1 (5- to 6-pound size) boned breast of veal	**Brine**
2 teaspoons salt	2 quarts water
1 teaspoon saltpeter	2 cups salt
1 teaspoon pepper	1 teaspoon saltpeter
1 teaspoon ground cloves	
1 teaspoon sugar	2 teaspoons unflavored gelatin
½ teaspoon ground allspice	½ cup cold water
½ pound salt pork, cut in ¼-inch slices	½ cup canned beef consomme, undiluted
3 tablespoons finely chopped onion	1 can (8-ounce size) whole carrots
2 tablespoons chopped fresh parsley	Parsley sprigs
	Lettuce leaves

1. Three or four days before serving: Wipe veal with damp paper towels. Trim off fat, and, if necessary, trim to make rectangular.

2. Combine 2 teaspoons salt, 1 teaspoon saltpeter, the pepper, cloves, sugar, and allspice; mix well. Sprinkle half of mixture over veal. Arrange saltpork slices evenly on veal, 1 inch from edges. Sprinkle with remaining spice mixture, the onion, and chopped parsley.

3. Roll up tightly, starting from short side. Close ends and side with skewers, and tie securely with twine. Then remove skewers.

4. Make brine: In large bowl, combine 2 quarts water, the salt, and saltpeter; stir until salt is dissolved.

5. Place veal roll in brine. Refrigerate, covered, 2 to 3 days. Turn meat once or twice each day.

6. To cook: Lift veal out of brine. Place in large kettle; cover with water. Bring to boiling; reduce heat, and simmer, covered, 1½ hours, or until veal is tender. Drain.

7. Place veal in a loaf pan. Set another loaf pan on top, and put in it a heavy object, such as a 5-pound bag of flour or sugar.

8. Refrigerate veal roll, weighted down, 24 hours.

9. Next day, in small saucepan, sprinkle gelatin over cold water, to soften—3 minutes. Heat over low heat, stirring, until gelatin is dissolved. Add to consomme in 1-cup measure. Refrigerate until it reaches the consistency of unbeaten egg white.

10. Remove veal to a small platter; remove twine. Brush all over with partially set gelatin mixture. Decorate with some of carrots, sliced, and parsley sprigs. Spoon on more gelatin mixture, to coat completely.

11. To serve: Arrange on platter. Cut some thin slices; garnish platter with whole carrots and crisp lettuce.

Makes 20 servings.

Jellied Veal and Pork

2 (1-pound size) veal shanks	16 whole black peppercorns
1 (2-pound size) boneless pork-shoulder roast	6 whole allspice
	4 whole cloves
6 cups water	2 bay leaves
2 medium onions, peeled and halved	1 envelope unflavored gelatin
	¼ cup cold water
2 medium carrots, pared and halved	2 tablespoons white vinegar
	½ teaspoon liquid
4 teaspoons salt	gravy seasoning

1. Wipe veal and pork with damp paper towels; remove any excess fat.

2. In large kettle, place 6 cups water, the meat, onions, carrots, salt, peppercorns, allspice, cloves, and bay leaves; bring to boiling.

3. Reduce heat, and simmer, covered, 2 to 2½ hours, or until meat is tender and veal practically falls from the bone. Lift veal and pork out of stock, and let cool.

4. Return stock to boiling, and cook, uncovered, until reduced to 3 cups. Strain into medium saucepan, and return to boiling.

5. Meanwhile, sprinkle gelatin over cold water; let stand 5 minutes to soften.

6. Add vinegar, gelatin, and gravy seasoning to boiling stock; stir until gelatin is dissolved. Cool quickly: Set saucepan of stock in large bowl of ice cubes; let stand, stirring occasionally, until consistency of unbeaten egg white—about 25 minutes.

7. Meanwhile, remove meat from veal shanks. Chop veal and pork—there should be about 5 cups (depends on amount of meat on veal shanks).

8. Combine chopped meat and chilled stock; mix well. Turn into oiled 9-by-5-by-3-inch loaf pan. Refrigerate, covered, until firm—at least 4 hours.

9. Unmold loaf: Run a small spatula around edge of pan; invert over platter, and shake gently to loosen. If necessary, put a hot, damp cloth over pan and shake again. Cut into slices about ½ inch thick. Serve with pickled beets (see p. 11) or curry dressing (see p. 47).

Makes 8 servings.

Veal Shoulder with Prune Stuffing

3 tablespoons butter or margarine	¼ teaspoon pepper
1 large onion, finely chopped	1 teaspoon dried tarragon or thyme leaves
1 small clove garlic, finely chopped	2 or 3 veal bones
2 cups fresh bread crumbs	1 small onion, peeled
1 can (8¾-ounce size) crushed pineapple, drained	2 cups dry white wine
¾ cup cooked prunes, pitted and diced	**Gravy**
1 (4- to 5-pound size) boned shoulder of veal, with pocket	2 cups pan juices
1 teaspoon salt	2 tablespoons butter or margarine
	3 tablespoons flour

1. In 2 tablespoons hot butter in small skillet, sauté the chopped onion and garlic until onion is golden. In medium bowl, add onion and garlic to crumbs, pineapple, and prunes. Toss to mix well.

2. Wipe veal well with damp paper towel. Rub with salt and pepper. Spoon stuffing into pocket. Roll up. Close with skewers or string.

3. In remaining butter, in 3-quart Dutch oven, brown roast well on all sides. Sprinkle with tarragon. Add veal bones, small onion, and wine. Reduce heat; cook, covered, 1½ to 2 hours, or until tender.

4. Place roast on hot platter; remove skewers or string. Keep hot.

5. Make gravy: Pour pan juices into small bowl of 1-quart measure. Skim off fat. Measure 2 cups juices. Melt butter in small saucepan. Remove from heat. Stir in flour and juices; bring to boiling, stirring. Serve with roast. Makes 8 servings.

Roast Saddle of Veal with Mushroom Sauce

1 (10- to 11-pound size) saddle of veal	Dash nutmeg
1 teaspoon salt	Dash pepper
¼ cup chopped fresh parsley	2 tablespoons olive oil
2 tablespoons chopped fresh chives	1 cup water
1 tablespoon chopped fresh tarragon	**Mushroom Sauce**
3 ounces salt pork for larding	3 tablespoons butter or margarine
½ cup finely chopped fresh mushrooms	1 cup chopped fresh mushrooms
2 tablespoons finely chopped shallot	3 tablespoons flour
	1½ cups pan drippings
	2 tablespoons Madeira

1. Wipe veal with damp paper towels. Place in shallow roasting pan without rack. Sprinkle with salt.

2. On sheet of waxed paper, combine parsley, chives, and tarragon. Cut salt pork into matchlike strips. Roll strips in herbs. With tip of sharp knife, make incisions in veal at about 1½-inch intervals. Insert salt-pork strips in incisions.

3. Place remaining herb mixture in medium bowl. Add ½ cup mushrooms, the shallot, nutmeg, pepper, and oil; mix well. Cover veal with this mixture, patting it on with hands. Cover loosely with foil; let stand about 3 hours.

4. Preheat oven to 350°F. Insert meat thermometer in center of thickest part of veal, away from bone. Roast 1 hour. Pour 1 cup water into roasting pan. Roast 2 to 2½ hours, or until thermometer registers 170°F.

5. Remove roast to platter, and keep warm. Pour pan drippings into a 2-cup measure; skim off fat. There should be about 1½ cups drippings (add water if necessary).

6. Make mushroom sauce: In hot butter in medium saucepan, sauté mushrooms until golden—about 5 minutes. Remove from heat; stir in

flour; gradually add pan drippings. Bring to boiling, stirring constantly, until sauce thickens; boil 2 minutes. Stir in Madeira.

7. To serve: Cut down to rib bones on each side of backbone. Then, using a long, thin-blade knife, cut along rib bones, following the curve so the fillet on each side is removed intact.

8. Slice each fillet into about 12 thin slices. Replace slices, overlapping, on bones. Place on large serving platter. When all slices have been served, remove the meat under the bones (tenderloin), and slice thinly.

9. If desired, garnish with sautéed whole mushrooms. Makes 12 servings.

Christmas Ham

2 teaspoons dried rosemary leaves	2 parsley sprigs
1½ teaspoons ground cloves	2 medium onions, peeled and sliced
1 teaspoon ground ginger	1 stalk celery with top, sliced
1 (10- to 12-pound size) fully cooked, bone-in whole ham	2 cups apple cider

1. Preheat oven to 325°F. Combine 1 teaspoon rosemary, 1 teaspoon cloves, and the ginger.

2. Place ham, fat side up, in shallow, open roasting pan. Rub surface with clove mixture. Insert meat thermometer in center, away from bone.

3. Place parsley, onion, and celery around ham; pour cider into pan. Cover pan tightly with foil.

4. Bake, basting every 20 minutes with cider mixture in pan, until thermometer registers 130°F.—about 3 hours. Remove from oven. Increase oven temperature to 400°F.

5. Pour off liquid from roasting pan, and strain. Skim off fat, and discard. Set liquid aside.

6. Remove ham skin, and score surface in diagonal pattern. Sprinkle with 1 teaspoon rosemary and ½ teaspoon cloves. Brush ham with some reserve liquid, being careful not to brush off rosemary.

7. Bake, uncovered and basting frequently and carefully with remaining liquid, about 30 minutes, or until browned. Remove ham to serving board or platter.

8. To serve: Carve a few slices, and arrange around ham. Garnish serving board with spiced crab apples, if desired.

Makes 30 to 40 buffet servings.

Roast Loin of Pork with Prunes

10 pitted dried prunes	½ teaspoon pepper
1 (4- to 4½-pound size)	3 tablespoons flour
pork loin	½ cup light cream or milk
1¾ teaspoons salt	1 teaspoon currant jelly

1. Preheat oven to 325°F. Soak prunes in hot water 30 minutes, to soften; drain well. Wipe pork with damp cloth. With sharp knife, make tiny slits between meat and bone; insert prunes. Then tie with twine, to hold the meat to the bone.

2. Combine 1 teaspoon salt, ¼ teaspoon pepper, and 1 tablespoon flour; rub into meat. Place, fat side up, in shallow roasting pan without rack. Insert meat thermometer in fleshy part, away from bone or fat. Roast, uncovered, 3 to 3½ hours, or to 185°F. on meat thermometer, for well done.

3. Remove pork to heated platter. For easier slicing, let stand in warm place 20 minutes before carving.

4. Meanwhile, make gravy: Pour pan drippings into 2-cup measure. Skim off fat; measure 2 tablespoons fat into roasting pan. Stir in flour until smooth. Add water to drippings to make 1¼ cups. Gradually stir into flour mixture, along with cream; bring to boiling, stirring. Add rest of salt and pepper and the currant jelly. Serve hot, with pork.

Makes 6 to 8 servings.

Roast Leg of Lamb

1 (4- to 4½-pound size)	1 tablespoon light cream
leg of lamb	2 teaspoons sugar
2 teaspoons salt	2 tablespoons flour
¼ teaspoon pepper	1½ cups milk
¾ cup black coffee	2 teaspoons currant jelly

1. Preheat oven to 350°F. Wipe lamb with damp cloth; rub with salt and pepper.

2. Place lamb, fat side up, on rack in shallow roasting pan. Insert meat thermometer in fleshy part, away from bone or fat. Roast, uncovered, 1½ hours.

3. Combine coffee, cream, and sugar; pour over lamb. Roast, basting occasionally, about 1 hour longer, or to 175°F. on meat thermometer for medium; 180°F. for well done. Remove lamb to heated platter. For easier slicing, let stand in warm place 20 minutes before carving.

4. Meanwhile, make gravy: Strain pan drippings. Skim off fat, and measure 2 tablespoons into roasting pan. Stir in flour until smooth; cook, stirring, over low heat about 1 minute, to brown flour slightly.

5. Pour pan drippings into 2-cup measure. Add enough milk to make 2 cups. Gradually stir into flour mixture; bring to boiling, stirring. Remove from heat; add currant jelly. Serve gravy hot, with lamb. Makes 6 to 8 servings.

POULTRY

Chicken in Aspic

1 (5-pound size) ready-to-cook roasting chicken	2 egg whites, slightly beaten
5 cups water	2 teaspoons lemon juice
2 large carrots, pared and halved	3 pimiento-stuffed olives, sliced
2 celery stalks, sliced	8 narrow pimiento strips, about 3 inches long
1 large onion	
4 whole cloves	Crisp salad greens
6 whole black peppercorns	2 medium-sized tomatoes, sliced
1 bay leaf	
1 tablespoon salt	½ pound fresh mushroom caps (optional)
2 envelopes unflavored gelatin	French dressing (optional)
½ cup cold water	Curry dressing (see p. 47)

1. Rinse chicken well under cold water. Place in large kettle with 5 cups water, the carrots, celery, onion, cloves, peppercorns, bay leaf, and salt; bring to boiling.

2. Reduce heat, and simmer, covered, 1 hour. Turn chicken over, and cook 1 hour longer, or until tender.

3. Lift chicken out of stock, and let cool. Strain stock; discard vegetables. Skim off fat. Measure stock; if necessary, boil, uncovered, to reduce to 1 quart.

4. Sprinkle gelatin over ½ cup cold water; let stand 5 minutes to soften. Add to stock in kettle along with egg whites; bring to boiling, stirring. Remove from heat; let stand 5 minutes.

5. Pour through large strainer, lined with double thickness of cheese-

cloth, into a large saucepan. Add lemon juice. Cool quickly: Set saucepan of stock in large bowl of ice cubes; let stand, stirring occasionally, until consistency of unbeaten egg white—about 25 minutes.

6. Pour ½ cup gelatin mixture into an oiled 2-quart mold or 2½-quart bowl. Add olive slices, arranging them decoratively. Brush side of mold with more gelatin mixture. Refrigerate until set—about 30 minutes.

7. Meanwhile, cut breast meat of chicken into thin, even slices. Remove rest of meat from bones, and cut into 1-inch pieces.

8. Dip sliced breast meat into gelatin mixture to coat lightly. Arrange with pimiento strips around inside of mold, overlapping slices as needed.

9. Add cut-up chicken to remaining gelatin mixture (if too stiff, heat just until melted); turn into center of mold. Refrigerate, covered, until firm—at least 4 hours.

10. To unmold: Run a small spatula around edge of mold; invert over platter, and shake gently to loosen. If necessary, put a hot, damp cloth over mold, and shake again.

11. Garnish with greens and tomato slices. Dip mushroom caps in French dressing, and arrange around mold. Serve with cold curry dressing. Makes 8 to 10 servings.

Curry Dressing

1 cup mayonnaise	1 tablespoon lemon juice
½ cup sour cream	2 teaspoons curry powder

1. In small bowl, combine all ingredients, mixing well. Refrigerate, covered, several hours, or until needed.

2. Turn into attractive dish. Serve with chicken in aspic. Makes 1½ cups.

Chicken with Wine and Cream

1 (3- to 4-pound size) chicken,	¼ pound butter
cut in serving pieces	2 cups white wine
Salt	1 cup cream
Pepper	½ cup blanched, slivered almonds

1. Preheat oven to 350°F. Sprinkle chicken with salt and pepper and brown it in butter in a large frying pan.

2. Transfer the chicken to a baking dish and bake, uncovered, for 30 minutes.

3. Turn off oven, remove chicken from the oven, and add the wine to the baking dish. Let the chicken steep in the wine for 1 hour.

4. Heat oven once again, this time to 300°F. Add the cream, stirring it in well, and return chicken to the oven for an additional 15 minutes. Remove, sprinkle with almonds, and serve.

Makes 6 servings.

Roast Goose Stuffed with Apples and Prunes

1 (10- to 12-pound size) goose	3 cups peeled, cored, and
½ onion	chopped apples
Salt and pepper	2 cups presoaked pitted and
	chopped dried prunes

1. Preheat oven to 325°F.

2. Wash goose under cold water, dry it with paper towels, and rub with onion inside and out.

3. Salt and pepper the inside of bird and stuff with the apples and prunes. Close the cavity with skewers, truss the bird, and roast it on a rack in a shallow open pan for 25 minutes per pound, drawing off goose fat with a bulb baster as it accumulates.

Makes 8 to 10 servings.

Sweet Breads & Pastries

The Scandinavians are among the world's finest bakers. During the long winters, with their early darkness, housewives traditionally kept their houses warm and their families intrigued with their endless experimentation at the oven. The most famous of Scandinavian pastries, the little sweet rolls we call Danish pastry, were developed only a hundred years ago through an intermarriage of the Danish and Viennese baking styles. But long before this, the Scandinavians were already famous for baking rolls and breads so flaky and rich they were considered choice gifts at holiday times. In Denmark it is customary to make miniature loaves of bread, wrap them, pan and all, on individual bread boards, and offer them as Christmas presents. In Sweden an entire holiday focuses around pastry: St. Lucia's Day, December 13. On the morning of St. Lucia's Day the daughters in Swedish families honor their parents with a ritual that all American mothers might envy. They go into the kitchen and bake a traditional saffron-flavored dough in the many imaginative shapes of St. Lucia buns. Then, donning long white dresses and wearing wreaths of lingonberries and candles in their hair, they present the pastries to their parents, serving them a delicious breakfast in bed of the pastries and hot coffee.

SWEET BREADS

Danish Almond Twist

Filling
½ cup butter or
margarine, melted
2 tablespoons sugar
1 package (4½-ounce size)
almond macaroons, crushed
½ teaspoon almond extract

¼ cup chopped toasted
almonds or walnuts

2 packages (8-ounce size)
refrigerator crescent rolls
1 egg white
1 tablespoon water
3 tablespoons sugar

1. Preheat oven to 375°F. Lightly grease a large cookie sheet.
2. Make filling: In small bowl, combine all filling ingredients; mix well.
3. Unroll one package of crescent-roll dough. On lightly floured surface, with hands, shape dough into a 16-by-10-inch rectangle. Press perforations together with fingertips.
4. Sprinkle rectangle with half of filling mixture. Roll up dough tightly, from long side, jelly-roll fashion. Pinch edge to seal.
5. Repeat with rest of dough and filling mixture.
6. Place rolls, side by side, on prepared cookie sheet. "Braid" rolls together. Then shape into a circle 9 inches in diameter. Pinch ends together to seal.
7. Beat egg white with water. Brush some of mixture over twist; sprinkle with 2 tablespoons sugar.
8. Bake 30 minutes, or until golden brown.
9. Brush with rest of egg-white mixture; sprinkle with remaining sugar. Cool slightly on wire rack. Serve warm, cut into wedges.
Makes 8 servings.

Swedish Tea Log

1 package active dry yeast
¼ cup warm water
2¼ cups unsifted
all-purpose flour
2 tablespoons granulated
sugar

1 teaspoon salt
½ cup butter or margarine
¼ cup evaporated milk,
undiluted
1 egg
¼ cup chopped dark raisins

Filling
¼ cup butter or margarine,
   softened
½ cup dark-brown sugar,
   firmly packed
½ cup chopped pecans
½ cup flaked coconut

Topping
2 tablespoons butter or
   margarine
1 cup confectioners' sugar
¼ cup evaporated milk,
   undiluted

1. Sprinkle yeast over water in small bowl, stirring until dissolved. Set aside.
2. In large bowl, combine flour, granulated sugar, and salt. With pastry blender, cut in ½ cup butter until mixture resembles coarse crumbs.
3. With wooden spoon, stir in ¼ cup milk, the egg, and raisins till well blended. Stir in yeast mixture.
4. Refrigerate, covered, overnight.
5. Next day, make filling: In medium bowl, combine ¼ cup softened butter, the brown sugar, pecans, and coconut; mix well.
6. Divide dough in half. On lightly floured surface, roll out one half into 12-by-9-inch rectangle. Spread with half of filling. Roll up, jelly-roll style, starting with long side. Place, seam side down, on greased cookie sheet. Repeat with rest of dough and filling.
7. Cover with towel; let rise in warm place (85°F.), free from drafts, until double in bulk—about 1 hour.
8. Preheat oven to 350°F. Bake logs 30 minutes, or until golden brown. Remove from cookie sheets; let cool slightly on wire rack.
9. Make topping: In small saucepan, slowly heat butter until golden brown. Remove from heat. Add sugar and milk; beat until smooth. Spread on logs while they are warm.
    Makes 2 logs.

Cardamom Wreath

1 cup warm water
   (105° to 115°F.)
2 packages active dry yeast
½ cup granulated sugar
1 teaspoon salt
¾ cup butter or
   margarine, softened
2 eggs

4¾ cups unsifted
   all-purpose flour
½ cup finely chopped citron
½ cup finely chopped
   candied cherries
½ cup dark raisins
½ cup coarsely chopped walnuts
¾ teaspoon crushed cardamom

2 tablespoons butter or
margarine, melted

3 tablespoons milk
½ teaspoon vanilla extract

Glaze
1½ cups confectioners' sugar

Candied cherries, halved
Citron

1. If possible, check temperature of warm water with thermometer. Sprinkle yeast over water in large bowl; stir until dissolved. Add granulated sugar and salt, stirring until dissolved.

2. Add soft butter, eggs, and 2½ cups flour; with electric mixer at medium speed, or vigorously with wooden spoon, beat until smooth—about 2 minutes.

3. Stir in ½ cup citron, ½ cup cherries, the raisins, nuts, and cardamom until well combined. Gradually add remaining flour, mixing with a wooden spoon or hands until dough is smooth and stiff enough to leave side of bowl.

4. Turn out dough onto lightly floured surface; roll to coat with flour. Cover with bowl; let rest 10 minutes; then knead until smooth—about 5 minutes.

5. Place in lightly greased large bowl; turn to bring greased side up. Cover with towel; let rise in warm place (85°F.), free from drafts, until double in bulk—about 2 hours.

6. Punch down dough; turn out onto lightly floured surface. Divide in thirds; with hands, roll each piece into a 24-inch-long strip.

7. Braid the 3 strips together. Place on a greased cookie sheet; form into a ring; pinch ends together to seal.

8. Cover with towel; let rise in warm place (85°F.), free from drafts, until double in bulk—about 1 hour.

9. Preheat oven to 375°F. Brush top of ring with 2 tablespoons melted butter.

10. Bake 40 to 45 minutes, or until nicely browned. Remove to wire rack, and let cool completely.

11. To store: Wrap ring in foil; seal, and label. Place in freezer.

12. To serve: Preheat oven to 400°F. Heat foil-wrapped frozen ring 30 to 35 minutes, or just until heated through.

13. Meanwhile, make glaze: In small bowl, mix sugar, milk, and vanilla until smooth. Unwrap ring, and place on wire rack. Brush with glaze, and decorate with candied cherries and citron.

Makes 12 servings.

Date-Nut Loaves

4 cups pitted dates
2 cups coarsely
  chopped walnuts
2 cups boiling water
3 cups unsifted all-
  purpose flour
1½ teaspoons baking soda
1 teaspoon salt

½ cup butter or
  margarine, softened
1¼ cups light-brown sugar,
  firmly packed
2 eggs
1 teaspoon vanilla extract

1. With scissors, cut dates into thirds into medium bowl. Add nuts and boiling water. Let cool to room temperature—about 45 minutes.

2. Meanwhile, grease four 5¾-by-3¼-by-2¼-inch loaf pans. Sift flour with baking soda and salt; set aside.

3. Preheat oven to 350°F.

4. In large bowl, with electric mixer at high speed, beat butter with sugar, eggs, and vanilla until ingredients are smooth.

5. Add cooled date mixture; mix well. Add flour mixture; beat with wooden spoon until well combined. Turn into prepared pans, dividing evenly.

6. Bake 1 hour, or until cake tester inserted in center comes out clean. Cool in pans 10 minutes; remove to wire rack, and let cool completely.

7. To store: Wrap each loaf in foil, plastic film, or moisture-vapor-proof freezer paper; seal, and label. Place in freezer.

8. To serve: Remove number of loaves desired from freezer. Let thaw, still in wrapping, at room temperature several hours, or until loaves are at room temperature.

Makes 4 small loaves.

Norwegian Christmas Bread

¾ cup milk
½ cup granulated sugar
¼ cup shortening
1½ teaspoons salt
2 packages active dry yeast
½ cup warm water
2 eggs, beaten
5 cups sifted all-
  purpose flour
1 teaspoon grated lemon peel

2 teaspoons ground cardamom
1½ cups diced mixed
  candied fruit
½ cup light raisins
¼ cup coarsely chopped walnuts

Icing
1 cup confectioners' sugar
1½ tablespoons milk

1. In small saucepan, heat ¾ cup milk just until bubbles form around edge of pan; remove from heat. Add granulated sugar, shortening, and salt, stirring until shortening is melted. Let cool to lukewarm.

2. Sprinkle yeast over water in large bowl, stirring until dissolved. Stir in milk mixture.

3. Add eggs, 2 cups flour, the lemon peel, and cardamom; beat with wooden spoon until smooth. Add candied fruit, raisins, and nuts. Stir in enough of remaining flour (2½ to 3 cups) to make a soft dough. Cover with towel; let rest 10 minutes.

4. Turn out dough onto lightly floured surface; knead until smooth and elastic—about 8 minutes.

5. Place in lightly greased, large bowl; turn to bring up greased side. Cover with towel; let rise in warm place (85°F.), free from drafts, until double in bulk—about 2 hours.

6. Punch down dough; divide in half. Shape each half into a ball. Cover, and let rest 10 minutes.

7. Pat each ball into 2 round loaves, and place on greased cookie sheets. Cover, and let rise until double in bulk—about 1½ hours.

8. Preheat oven to 350°F. Bake loaves 20 minutes; place piece of foil over top of each loaf. Bake 25 minutes longer, or until deep golden brown.

9. Remove from cookie sheets; let cool on wire rack.

10. Make icing: In small bowl, mix sugar with milk until smooth. Brush over loaves while they're still slightly warm. If desired, decorate with walnuts and bits of candied fruit.

Makes 4 loaves.

PASTRY

Danish Pastry

1½ cups butter or margarine, slightly softened (¾ pound)	2 packages active dry yeast
3¾ cups unsifted all-purpose flour	1 egg
½ cup warm water (105° to 115°F.)	¾ cup cold milk
	⅓ cup sugar
	½ teaspoon salt

1. In medium bowl, with wooden spoon, cream butter until smooth. Add ¼ cup flour; stir until well blended.

2. Place on sheet of waxed paper on a damp surface, and cover with a

second sheet. With rolling pin, roll to an 11-by-9-inch rectangle. (See illustration 1.) Refrigerate 20 to 30 minutes, or until well chilled.

3. Meanwhile, if possible, check temperature of warm water with thermometer. Sprinkle yeast over warm water in large bowl, stirring until dissolved. Add egg, milk, sugar, and salt; mix until well blended.

4. With wooden spoon, beat in 3 cups flour; continue to beat until smooth and elastic—about 5 minutes. (See illustration 2.) Stir in remaining ½ cup flour, and beat 2 minutes longer. Dough will be soft.

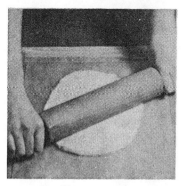

Illustration 1   *Illustration 2*

5. Refrigerate dough, covered, 10 minutes.

6. Sprinkle pastry cloth or board generously with flour. Turn dough onto cloth; dough will be soft. Sprinkle with more flour. (Use no more than ¼ cup flour in all for sprinkling.) Pat with hands or roll out into a 14-by-12-inch rectangle. Brush off excess flour with soft pastry brush.

7. Peel top sheet of waxed paper from chilled butter rectangle. Invert over dough ½ inch in from one end, leaving ½-inch margin on sides. Butter will cover about two thirds of dough rectangle. Peel off paper. (See illustration 3, next page.) Starting with unbuttered third, fold dough in thirds, making 3 layers. (See illustration 4, next page.) As you fold dough, brush off excess flour with pastry brush.

8. Turn dough with folded side at right; then, starting from center, roll out into a 14-by-12-inch rectangle. (See illustration 5, next page.) If butter breaks through, brush spot very lightly with flour. From short side, fold dough into thirds. Carefully lift onto a cookie sheet; cover with foil. Refrigerate 15 minutes.

9. Repeat rolling, folding, and chilling dough 3 more times (4 times in all).

10. Keep dough refrigerated until ready to roll and shape as below.

Illustration 3

Illustration 4

Illustration 5

Cockscombs

Almond Filling   1 recipe for Danish
 1 egg white   pastry (see pp. 54–56)
 ½ cup almond paste 1 egg, slightly beaten
 ⅔ cup confectioners' sugar Granulated sugar

1. Make almond filling: In small bowl, slightly beat egg white. Add almond paste and confectioners' sugar; stir with fork until smooth. Set aside.

2. Lightly grease 2 large cookie sheets. Remove pastry from refrigerator.

3. On floured surface, roll pastry into an 18-by-16-inch rectangle. Cut lengthwise into 4 strips.

4. Spread about 2 tablespoons filling down center of each strip. Fold one side of dough over filling, and press to other side to seal.

5. Cut each strip crosswise into thirds. Cut 7 slits, ¾ inch deep, in sealed edge of each piece. (See illustration following.) Place, 4 inches apart, on prepared cookie sheets. Curve each piece to separate slits.

Cockscombs   *Cut slits in sealed edge*

6. Cover with foil or plastic film. Refrigerate overnight.

7. To bake: Preheat oven to 400°F. Remove cockscombs from refrigerator; uncover. Brush with egg; then sprinkle generously with granulated sugar.

8. Bake 5 minutes. Reduce oven temperature to 350°F.; bake 15 minutes longer, or until puffed and golden brown.

9. Remove from cookie sheets to wire rack. Serve warm.
Makes 1 dozen.

Pinwheels

1 cup apricot or prune filling (see p. 58)	1 egg, slightly beaten
1 recipe Danish pastry (see pp. 54–56)	Glaze (see p. 59) (optional)

1. Make either apricot or prune filling.

2. Lightly grease 2 large cookie sheets. Remove pastry from refrigerator.

3. On floured surface, roll pastry into an 18-inch square. Cut into 4

squares. Place 2 squares on each prepared cookie sheet. Then, if necessary, roll each again, to make 9-inch square.

4. In each square, make a 4-inch slit from each corner toward center. Place 1 tablespoon filling on pastry between each two slits. Then fold every other point of corners toward center, partially covering filling and forming a pinwheel. (See illustration.) Moisten points with a little water; press gently to seal.

5. Cover with foil or plastic film. Refrigerate overnight.

6. To bake: Preheat oven to 400°F. Remove pinwheels from refrigerator; uncover. Brush top of each pinwheel with egg.

7. Bake 5 minutes. Reduce oven temperature to 350°F.; bake 25 to 30 minutes longer, or until puffed and golden brown.

8. Remove from cookie sheets to wire rack. Drizzle with glaze. Serve warm.

Makes 4 large pinwheels, 16 servings.

Pinwheel

Fold point of corner to center

Apricot or Prune Filling

1 cup dried apricots or pitted prunes	⅔ cup water ⅓ cup sugar

1. In small saucepan, place apricots or prunes and ⅔ cup water. Bring to boiling; reduce heat, and simmer, covered, 30 minutes.

2. Cool. Then mash fruit or chop finely. Stir in sugar. Refrigerate, covered, until well chilled—at least 1 hour.

Makes 1 cup.

Glaze

½ cup confectioners' sugar   2½ teaspoons milk

In small bowl, mix sugar with milk until smooth. If glaze seems too thick, add a little more milk. Makes about ¼ cup.

Envelopes

1 cup apricot or prune   1 egg, slightly beaten
  filling (see p. 58)   Confectioners' sugar
1 recipe Danish pastry
  (see pp. 54–56)

1. Make either apricot or prune filling.
2. Lightly grease 2 large cookie sheets. Remove pastry from refrigerator.
3. On floured surface, roll out pastry into an 18-inch square. Cut into 4 squares.
4. Place 2 tablespoons filling on each of two opposite corners of each square; spread slightly. Then fold over other two corners to partially cover filling, overlapping corners. (See illustration.) Place 2 envelopes, 4 inches apart, on each prepared cookie sheet.
5. Cover with foil or plastic film. Refrigerate overnight.
6. To bake: Preheat oven to 400°F. Remove envelopes from refrigerator; uncover. Brush top of each envelope with egg.

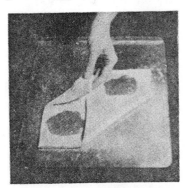

Envelope   *Fold over corners of square*

7. Bake 5 minutes. Reduce oven temperature to 350°F.; bake 25 to 30 minutes longer, or until puffed and golden brown.

8. Remove from cookie sheets to wire rack. Sprinkle with confectioners' sugar. Serve warm.

Makes 4 large envelopes, 8 servings.

Kringle

Cardamom Filling	½ recipe Danish pastry
6 tablespoons butter, softened	(see pp. 54–56)
¾ cup confectioners' sugar	1 egg, slightly beaten
½ cup currants	3 tablespoons granulated sugar
½ teaspoon ground cardamom	Glaze (see p. 59)

1. Make cardamom filling: In small bowl, cream butter with confectioners' sugar until fluffy. Stir in currants and cardamom. Set aside.

2. Lightly grease a large cookie sheet. Remove pastry from refrigerator.

3. On floured surface, roll pastry into a 40-inch-long strip, 6 inches wide. Spread filling in a narrow line down center of strip. Fold one side over filling, just to cover it; then fold over other side, overlapping about ¾ inch. Moisten edge with a little water; press gently to seal. Then pinch ends to seal.

4. Carefully lift pastry, seam side up, onto prepared cookie sheet, and gently form it into a pretzel shape. (See illustration.)

5. Cover with foil or plastic film. Refrigerate overnight.

6. To bake: Preheat oven to 400°F. Remove kringle from refrigerator; uncover. Brush top with egg; then sprinkle with granulated sugar.

Kringle

Form into pretzel shape

7. Bake 5 minutes. Reduce oven temperature to 350°F.; bake 25 minutes longer, or until puffed and golden brown.

8. Remove from cookie sheet to wire rack. Let cool slightly while making glaze. Drizzle with glaze. Serve warm.

Makes 12 servings.

Mayor's Braids

Macaroon Filling	½ teaspoon almond extract
½ cup butter or margarine,	1 recipe Danish pastry
softened	(see pp. 54–56)
1 cup confectioners' sugar	1 egg, slightly beaten
½ cup finely crushed	2 tablespoons granulated sugar
almond macaroons	¼ cup sliced blanched almonds

1. Make macaroon filling: In small bowl, cream butter with confectioners' sugar until fluffy. Stir in macaroons and almond extract. Set aside.

2. Lightly grease 2 large cookie sheets. Remove pastry from refrigerator.

3. On floured surface, roll out pastry to an 18-by-14-inch rectangle. Cut in half lengthwise; cut each half lengthwise into thirds, making 6 strips in all.

Mayor's Braid   *Press together at one end; braid*

4. Spread about 2 tablespoons filling down center of each strip. Fold edges over filling, and pinch together to seal.

5. For each braid, place 3 strips, seam side down, on a prepared cookie sheet. Press together at one end; braid loosely (see illustration); then press ends together to seal.

6. Cover with foil or plastic film. Refrigerate overnight.

7. To bake: Preheat oven to 400°F. Remove braids from refrigerator; uncover. Brush top of each braid with egg. Sprinkle each with 1 tablespoon granulated sugar and 2 tablespoons almonds.

8. Bake 5 minutes. Reduce oven temperature to 350°F.; bake 35 minutes longer, or until puffed and golden brown.

9. Remove from cookie sheets to wire rack to cool. Serve warm. Makes 2 braids, 24 servings.

Pecan Ring

Pecan Filling
¼ cup butter or margarine, softened
½ cup confectioners' sugar
½ cup chopped pecans
1 teaspoon rum extract

½ recipe Danish pastry (see pp. 54–56)
1 egg, slightly beaten
Glaze (see p. 59)

1. Make pecan filling: In small bowl, cream butter with sugar until fluffy. Stir in pecans and rum extract. Set aside.

Pecan Ring

Place slices on pastry in mold

2. Lightly grease a 6-cup ring mold and 5 (2½-inch) muffin-pan cups. Remove pastry from refrigerator.

3. On floured surface, roll pastry into a 14-inch square. From one side, cut two 3-inch-wide strips, and fit into bottom of prepared ring mold. Spread with ¼ cup filling.

4. Spread remaining filling on pastry rectangle on work surface. Roll up, starting from long side, like a jelly roll. Cut roll crosswise into 14

(1-inch) slices. Place 9 slices, cut side up, on pastry in ring mold. (See illustration.) Place remaining slices, cut side up, in prepared muffin-pan cups.

5. Cover with foil or plastic film. Refrigerate overnight.
6. To bake: Preheat oven to 400°F. Remove ring and rolls from refrigerator; uncover. Brush with egg.
7. Bake 5 minutes. Reduce oven temperature to 350°F.; bake ring 35 minutes, or until puffed and golden brown; muffin-pan cups, 20 minutes.
8. Let cool in pans on wire rack 5 minutes. Invert onto wire rack; turn right side up. Drizzle glaze on rolls and ring, as shown in illustration. Serve warm.

Makes 1 ring and 5 rolls.

Danish Strip

1 cup apricot filling (see p. 58) or raspberry jam	½ teaspoon vanilla extract
	1 recipe Danish pastry (see pp. 54–56)
Butter Cream	
¼ cup butter or margarine, softened	1 egg, slightly beaten
½ cup confectioners' sugar	¼ cup granulated sugar

1. Make apricot filling.

2. Make butter cream: In small bowl, cream butter with confectioners' sugar until fluffy. Stir in vanilla. Set aside.

3. Lightly grease 2 large cookie sheets. Remove pastry from refrigerator; divide in half.

4. On floured surface, roll out half of pastry into a 16-by-12-inch rectangle. Cut in half lengthwise.

5. Spread about 2 tablespoons butter cream down center of each strip; then top with ¼ cup filling or jam. Fold one side over filling, just to cover it. Then fold over other side, overlapping about ¾ inch; press gently to seal. Place, 4 inches apart, on prepared cookie sheet. Repeat with other half of dough.

6. Cover with foil or plastic film. Refrigerate overnight.

7. To bake: Preheat oven to 400°F. Remove strips from refrigerator; uncover. Brush top of each strip with egg; sprinkle with 1 tablespoon granulated sugar.

8. Bake 5 minutes. Reduce oven temperature to 350°F.; bake 20 to 25 minutes longer, or until puffed and golden brown.

9. Remove from cookie sheets to wire rack to cool. Serve warm. Makes 4 strips, 24 servings.

Miniature Danish Pastries

1 package (14-ounce size)
refrigerator turnover pastries
(cherry, blueberry, or
apple fillings)

1 egg yolk

1. Preheat oven to 400°F. Separate half of dough into 4 squares; refrigerate remaining dough.

2. On lightly floured surface, fold each square of dough in half. Roll each into a 5-by-2½-inch rectangle. Cut each rectangle in half to make two 2½-inch squares. Repeat with remaining squares and with other half of dough, making 16 squares in all.

3. Shape and fill as directed below. Place on ungreased cookie sheet.

4. Beat egg yolk with 1 teaspoon water. Brush over pastries. Bake 10 minutes, or until golden brown. Serve warm from the oven. Makes 16 miniature pastries.

How to Shape and Fill Miniature Danish Pastries

Pinwheels:

Use a 2½-inch pastry square. Make cuts from tip of each corner to within ½ inch of the center. Squeeze about 1 teaspoon filling in center of each. Bring alternate points to the center; moisten slightly, and press together.

Diamonds:

Use a 2½-inch pastry square. Squeeze about 1 teaspoon filling in center. Bring two opposite corners to center; moisten slightly, and press edges together.

Tartlets:

Use a 2½-inch pastry square. Squeeze about 1 teaspoon filling in center. Bring four corners to center, and press edges together (corners will open slightly during baking).

Warm Cheese Danish Pastry

1 package (3-ounce size)
cream cheese
1 egg yolk

2 tablespoons orange
marmalade
1 teaspoon flour

1 package (8-ounce size) refrigerated crescent dinner rolls	Confectioners' sugar Cherry preserves

1. Preheat oven to 375°F.
2. In small bowl, combine cheese, egg yolk, marmalade, and flour. Beat with electric mixer or rotary beater until almost smooth.
3. See illustrations. Carefully unroll dough, and separate into 8 triangles. Lay one triangle with the long side parallel with end of a large cookie sheet. Place next triangle overlapping first and with point in opposite direction. Continue in this way until all are used, making a 16-inch length. Dough will be solid about 3 inches wide down center.
4. Spoon cheese mixture over the center. Fold points over the filling.
5. Bake 15 minutes, or until golden brown.
6. Cool 5 minutes. Sprinkle with confectioners' sugar. Spoon cherry preserves over top. Serve warm.

Makes 8 servings.

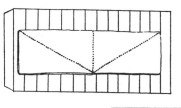
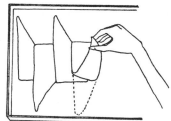
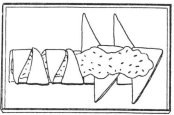

Swedish Christmas Buns

Saffron Dough*	1 teaspoon salt
1 cup milk	½ cup butter or margarine,
¼ to ½ teaspoon crumbled	softened
saffron threads, or	¾ cup warm water
½ teaspoon powdered saffron	(110° to 115°F.)
¾ cup sugar	2 packages active dry yeast

* *Cardamom dough: Substitute ½ to 1 teaspoon ground cardamom and 1 tablespoon grated orange rind for the saffron.*

6½ cups sifted all-
    purpose flour
2 eggs

½ cup dark raisins
½ cup ground blanched almonds

1. In small saucepan, heat milk just until bubbles form around edge of pan. Remove from heat. Add saffron, sugar, salt, and butter, stirring until butter is melted. Let cool to lukewarm.

2. If possible, check temperature of warm water with thermometer. Sprinkle yeast over it in large bowl, stirring until dissolved. Stir in milk mixture.

3. Add 3½ cups flour; beat with wooden spoon until smooth—about 2 minutes. Beat in eggs, dark raisins, and the almonds. Then gradually add the remaining flour, mixing in last of it with hand until the dough leaves side of bowl. (This is soft dough.)

4. Turn out dough onto lightly floured pastry cloth. Cover with bowl; let rest for 10 minutes. Turn over the dough, to coat with flour; knead until it is smooth—about 5 minutes.

5. Place in lightly greased large bowl; turn, to bring up greased side. Cover with towel; let rise in warm place (85°F.), free from drafts, until double in bulk—1 to 1½ hours. Punch down. Turn out onto lightly floured pastry cloth.

6. Divide and shape as directed for wagon wheels, Joseph's beard, twists, candle braid, crown of the Virgin, St. Lucia buns, goat, Star of Bethlehem, or wheel of cart. The following recipe directions are for one-third of dough—enough to work with at a time.

Wagon Wheels

1. On lightly floured pastry cloth, with hands, shape one-third of dough into a 12-inch roll. Cut into 10 pieces. Cut each in half; with palms, roll each into pencil-thin strip, 10 inches long.

2. On greased large cookie sheet, place 2 strips, side by side; pinch together in center; coil ends as in diagram. Press a raisin in center of each coil.

3. Cover with towel; let rise in warm place (85°F.), free from drafts, until double in bulk—40 to 50 minutes.

4. Meanwhile, preheat oven to 400°F. Brush wheels with an egg yolk mixed with 1 tablespoon water; bake 12 to 15 minutes, or until golden brown. Cool on wire rack.

Makes 10.

Wagon Wheels

Joseph's Beard

1. On lightly floured pastry cloth, with hands, shape one-third of the dough into a 12-inch roll. Cut into 10 pieces; cut each piece into thirds.
2. Use 3 pieces to make each beard. With palms, roll one into 10-inch pencil-thin strip, one into 8-inch strip, one into 6-inch strip.
3. On greased large cookie sheet, bend 10-inch strip into U-shape; place 8-inch strip inside 10-inch strip, 6-inch strip inside 8-inch strip; coil all ends as in diagram. Press a raisin in center of each coil.
4. Cover with towel; let rise in warm place (85°F.), free from drafts, till double in bulk—40 to 50 minutes.
5. Meanwhile, preheat oven to 400°F. Brush beards with an egg yolk mixed with 1 tablespoon water; bake 12 to 15 minutes, or until golden brown. Cool on wire rack.

Makes 10.

Joseph's Beard

Twists

1. On lightly floured pastry cloth, with hands, shape one-third of dough into a 12-inch roll. Cut into 12 pieces.
2. With palms, roll each into a pencil-thin strip, 8 inches long. Place on greased large cookie sheet.

3. Shape each into an S; coil ends as in diagram. Press a raisin in center of each coil.

4. Cover with towel; let rise in warm place (85°F.), free from drafts, until double in bulk—40 to 50 minutes.

5. Meanwhile, preheat oven to 400°F. Brush twists with an egg yolk mixed with 1 tablespoon water; bake 12 to 15 minutes, or until golden brown. Cool on wire rack.

Makes 12.

Twists

Candle Braid

1. On lightly floured pastry cloth, divide one-third of dough into 3 parts. With hands, shape each into a 20-inch roll.

2. Place on lightly greased large cookie sheet. Braid loosely. Shape braid into a circle; pinch ends together, to seal.

3. To make holes for candles, insert 7 balls of aluminum foil, 1 inch in diameter, between strands of braid, spacing evenly.

4. Cover with towel; let rise in warm place (85°F.), free from drafts, until double in bulk—about 60 minutes.

5. Meanwhile, preheat oven to 375°F. Bake braid 10 minutes.

6. Remove from oven; take out balls. Brush braid with an egg white mixed with 1 tablespoon water; sprinkle with 1 tablespoon sugar and 2 tablespoons ground almonds.

7. Continue baking 20 to 25 minutes, or until golden brown. Cool on wire rack.

8. Before serving, stand 7-inch red or white candles in holes. Light before bringing to the table.

Makes 1 braided ring.

Note: Instead of being brushed with egg-white mixture, the candle braid may be baked 30 to 35 minutes, cooled slightly, and frosted with this icing: Mix 2 cups sifted confectioners' sugar with 2 tablespoons milk. Decorate frosted braid with chopped candied red cherries and green citron or angelica.

Candle Braid

Crown of the Virgin

1. On lightly floured pastry cloth, with hands, shape one-third of the dough into 12-inch roll. Cut into 8 pieces; cut each in half.

2. With palms, roll 8 pieces into pencil-thin strips, 15 inches long. Cut each into thirds.

3. Make 8 braids; pinch ends to seal.

4. Place on greased large cookie sheet. Roll remaining 8 pieces into pencil-thin strips, 10 inches long. Cut each into fifths. Tuck ends of 5 strips under each braid; coil other ends. Press a raisin in center of each coil.

5. Cover with towel; let rise in warm place (85°F.), free from drafts, until double in bulk—40 to 50 minutes.

6. Meanwhile, preheat oven to 400°F. Brush crowns with an egg yolk mixed with 1 tablespoon water; bake 12 to 15 minutes, or until golden brown. Cool on wire rack.

Makes 8.

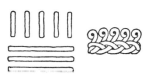

Crown of the Virgin

St. Lucia Buns

1. On lightly floured pastry cloth, roll one-third of dough into a 10-inch square. Cut in half to make two 10-by-5-inch rectangles; cut each rectangle crosswise into 12 strips.

2. With palm, roll each into a pencil-thin strip, 6 inches long. On lightly greased large cookie sheet, cross 2 strips to make an X; curl each end into a small coil. Press a raisin in center of each coil.

3. Cover with towel; let rise in warm place (85°F.), free from drafts, until double in bulk—40 to 50 minutes.

4. Meanwhile, preheat oven to 400°F. Brush buns with an egg yolk mixed with 1 tablespoon water; bake 12 to 15 minutes, or until golden brown. Cool on wire rack.

Makes 12.

St. Lucia Buns

Goat

1. On lightly floured pastry cloth, roll one-third of dough into an 8-inch square. Cut in half to make two 8-by-4-inch rectangles; cut each rectangle into 6 strips.

2. With palms, roll each into a pencil-thin strip, 11 inches long. Place on lightly greased large cookie sheet. Bend each strip in center; coil 2 ends to make horns. Press a raisin in center of each coil.

3. Cover with towel; then let rise in warm place (85°F.), free from drafts, until double in bulk—40 to 50 minutes.

4. Meanwhile, preheat oven to 400°F. Brush buns with an egg yolk mixed with 1 tablespoon water; bake 12 to 15 minutes, or until golden brown. Cool on wire rack.

Makes 12.

Goat

Star of Bethlehem

1. On lightly floured pastry cloth, shape one-third of dough, with hands, into a 12-inch roll. Cut into 24 pieces.

2. With palms, roll each into a pencil-thin strip, 10 inches long. Form each into triangle; pinch ends together. Place 12 triangles on greased large cookie sheet. Top with rest of triangles, to make 6-pointed stars.

3. Cover with towel; let rise in warm place (85°F.), free from drafts, until double in bulk—40 to 50 minutes.

4. Meanwhile, preheat oven to 400°F. Brush stars with an egg yolk mixed with 1 tablespoon water; bake 12 to 15 minutes, or until golden brown. Cool on wire rack.

Makes 12.

Star of Bethlehem

Wheel of Cart

1. On lightly floured pastry cloth, shape one-third of dough, with hands, into a 10-inch roll. Cut into 10 pieces; cut each piece into 6 parts.

2. With palm, roll each into a pencil-thin strip, 4 inches long. Use 6 strips for each wheel. On lightly greased large cookie sheet, arrange 6 strips like spokes of a wheel. Press down center to seal; coil ends as in diagram. Press a raisin in center of each coil.

3. Cover with towel; let rise in warm place (85°F.), free from drafts, until double in bulk—takes about 40 to 50 minutes.

4. Meanwhile, preheat oven to 400°F. Brush wheels with an egg yolk mixed with 1 tablespoon water; bake 12 to 15 minutes, or until golden brown. Cool on wire rack.

Makes 10.

Wheel of Cart

Candy, Cake, & Cookies

Once upon a time in Sweden, it was a custom at birthdays for the housewife to bake seven different kinds of cookies. In Finland, the birthday cookie requirement was for only four different kinds, but the lady of the house also had to provide two simple cakes and one elaborate filled one for the celebration.

Even though today's Scandinavian housewives are no longer compelled by custom to produce so many cakes and cookies at once, they still do. At meal's end, accompanied by coffee, there always appears a delicious array of goodies. Among them, there may be relatively simple cakes, such as Icelandic torte, or great towering works of art, such as Danish almond ring, or delectable cookies, such as Finnish logs, almond lace wafers, and Upsala holiday cookies, and gingerbread. But there will never be just one sweet—the Scandinavians are too dedicated to pleasing guests to impose a single dessert on them. In choosing among the sweets in this chapter for a dinner party, try to think Scandinavian: choose two cookie recipes, or Swedish pancakes and some cookies, or a cake and cookies. It is a most generous way to close a meal.

CANDY

Candied Lemon Peel

5 large lemons (2 pounds)	¼ cup light corn syrup
3 cups sugar	6 drops yellow food coloring

1. Cut lemons in half lengthwise; squeeze out as much juice as possible. Refrigerate juice to use as desired.

2. In heavy, 3-quart saucepan, place peel and 2 quarts water; bring to boiling. Reduce heat, and simmer, covered, 30 to 40 minutes, or until peel is tender.

3. Drain; cool slightly. Carefully scrape excess pulp from peel.

4. In same saucepan, combine 1 cup water, 2 cups sugar, the corn syrup, and food coloring. Cook over medium heat, stirring constantly, until sugar is dissolved and syrup comes to boiling. Continue cooking, without stirring, to 235°F. on candy thermometer, or until a little in cold water forms a soft ball.

5. Add lemon peel; simmer gently, stirring frequently, 30 to 40 minutes, or until peel becomes translucent. (To prevent scorching during cooking, lift peel off bottom of pan several times.)

6. Turn peel and syrup into bowl. Let stand in a cool, dry place, covered, overnight.

7. Next day, remove peel from syrup to wire rack, and let drain 3 hours. Then, with scissors, cut into ¼-inch-wide strips. Roll in remaining sugar, coating well. Place on rack to partially dry—about 3 hours. Roll in sugar again.

8. Store peel in a tightly covered container.

Makes about 1 pound.

Burnt Almond Candy

1⅓ cups almonds, with skins on	1 cup sugar
	1 cup water

1. In heavy, medium skillet, combine almonds, sugar, and 1 cup water. Bring to boiling, stirring until sugar melts. Reduce heat; simmer until almonds make a popping sound—15 to 20 minutes.

2. Remove from heat. Stir until sugar crystallizes (mixture will become dry).

3. Return to heat; cook over low to medium heat until sugar starts to melt and clings to almonds, forming a glaze—15 minutes.

4. Turn out onto a greased cookie sheet to cool. Separate almonds with a fork. Cool completely. Store in container with tight-fitting lid in a cool, dry place.

Makes about 2 cups.

Hazelnut Truffles

¾ cup hazelnuts
6 squares (1-ounce size) semisweet chocolate
⅓ cup heavy cream

1⅓ cups confectioners' sugar
1 egg white
1 tablespoon Grand Marnier, Cointreau, or rum

1. Grind hazelnuts in a blender or in a Mouli grater. Line bottom of a 9-by-5-by-3-inch loaf pan with waxed paper.

2. In small, heavy saucepan, combine chocolate and cream. Heat over low heat just until chocolate is melted. Remove from heat.

3. In medium bowl, combine nuts, sugar, and egg white. With wooden spoon, stir until combined. Stir in chocolate mixture and liqueur to combine well.

4. Turn into prepared pan, or use to fill fluted paper bonbon cups. Refrigerate until firm. Cut into ¾-inch squares. Store, covered, in refrigerator.

Makes about 60 pieces.

CAKE

Swedish Pancakes

1¼ cups sifted all-purpose flour
2 tablespoons sugar
½ teaspoon salt
3 eggs
3 cups milk
¼ cup butter or margarine, melted

Salad oil
1 jar (14¾-ounce size) lingonberries, undrained; or
1 can (1-pound size) jellied whole-cranberry sauce

1. Sift flour with sugar and salt into medium bowl. With rotary beater, beat in eggs, milk, and butter until mixture is smooth.

2. Slowly heat Swedish iron pancake pan (or heavy frying pan or griddle) until a drop of water will sizzle and roll off. Brush lightly with oil.

3. Stir batter just before using. Pour 1 tablespoonful into each section of pancake pan, tilting pan so batter covers each section completely. (Or use 1 tablespoon batter per pancake in frying pan or griddle.)

4. When surface of pancake bubbles, turn quickly, and brown other side. Keep warm while rest of pancakes cook.

5. Meanwhile, heat the lingonberries slightly. Serve warm, with pancakes.

Makes 54 pancakes, each 3 inches in diameter—8 to 10 servings.

Cornucopia

4 cans (8-ounce size)	Frosting
almond paste*	1 egg white
2 cups granulated sugar	1 cup confectioners' sugar
½ cup egg whites (about 3)	½ teaspoon white vinegar
Confectioners' sugar	

1. In top of double boiler, combine almond paste, granulated sugar, and ½ cup egg whites.

2. Place over hot water; stir constantly with a wooden spoon until mixture is warm and smooth. Remove top of double boiler from water; let cool about 10 minutes.

3. Grease and flour 2 or 3 large cookie sheets.

4. Turn almond mixture onto board sprinkled lightly with confectioners' sugar. Knead 2 or 3 minutes, or until smooth.

5. Keeping hands and work surface coated with confectioners' sugar, shape some of dough into a ½-inch-thick rope 4 inches long. Make 13 more ropes, each 1½ inches longer than the preceding rope. Shape each into a ring, pinching ends together. Place on cookie sheets, fitting a small ring inside a large one and allowing 2 inches between. Refrigerate 30 minutes.

6. Preheat oven to 325°F. Bake rings 15 to 20 minutes, or until a light golden. Place cookie sheets on wire racks; cool 15 minutes. With spatula, loosen rings carefully, and remove to wire racks; let cool completely.

7. Make frosting: Place egg white, sugar, and vinegar in small bowl.

* *Do not use prepared almond filling instead of almond paste.*

With electric mixer at medium speed, beat until soft peaks form when beater is slowly raised. Place in pastry bag with writing tip.

8. To decorate rings: Pipe frosting in zigzag fashion on each ring. Let stand about 1 hour, or until icing is dry. Rings may then be stored in tightly covered container for several days before making into a cornucopia.

9. To make cornucopia: Tear off a piece of heavy-duty aluminum foil, 18 by 24 inches. Roll it, on the diagonal, into a cone about 7½ inches across at open end. Fasten with transparent tape. With hand inside cone, place the cookie rings on the form, starting with largest ring, then next largest, and ending with smallest. Squeeze foil if necessary, so rings touch and foil does not show.

10. Lay cornucopia on a large serving tray, propping up the narrow end with an apple. Cut off any foil that shows at open end.

11. Fill with sweets and fruits to use as a holiday centerpiece and dessert.

Icelandic Torte

Filling
2 packages (12-ounce size) pitted dried prunes
2 cups water
¾ cup granulated sugar
1 teaspoon vanilla extract
¾ teaspoon crushed cardamom seed
¼ teaspoon salt

Torte Layers
4 cups sifted all-purpose flour

2 teaspoons baking powder
½ teaspoon salt
1 cup butter or margarine, softened
1 cup granulated sugar
1 teaspoon vanilla extract
2 eggs
¼ cup milk

Confectioners' sugar
Whipped cream

1. Make filling: In 3-quart saucepan, place prunes and 2 cups water; bring to boiling. Reduce heat, and simmer, covered, 30 minutes, or until prunes are very tender.

2. Drain prunes, reserving liquid. Chop prunes finely. Add ¾ cup granulated sugar, 1 teaspoon vanilla, the cardamom, ¼ teaspoon salt, and ½ cup reserved cooking liquid; mix until ingredients are well blended. Set aside to cool.

3. Make torte layers: Sift flour with baking powder and salt.

4. In large bowl, with electric mixer at high speed, beat butter with granulated sugar and vanilla until light and fluffy.

5. Add eggs, one at a time, beating well after each addition.

6. At low speed, add flour mixture alternately with milk, beginning and ending with flour mixture.

7. Refrigerate dough until chilled and easy to handle—about 20 minutes.

8. Preheat oven to 350°F. Divide dough into 7 equal pieces.

9. For each layer, invert an 8-inch round layer-cake pan. Flatten a piece of dough with hands; place on pan; pat to fit. Then gently roll to make layer even; trim edge if necessary. Keep pieces of dough refrigerated until ready to use.

10. Bake 15 to 20 minutes, or until edge is golden brown. Carefully remove to wire rack; let cool.

11. To assemble: Place one layer on serving plate; spread with about ½ cup filling. Repeat with 5 more layers and remaining filling. Set last layer on top. Cover completely with plastic film or foil.

12. Refrigerate at least 24 hours, to mellow.

13. To serve: Sprinkle top with confectioners' sugar. Cut in thin slices. Pass whipped cream. Return unused portion to refrigerator.

Makes 16 servings.

Harvest Fruitcake

Fruit Mixture
1½ cups currants
1 package (10-ounce size) light raisins
½ pound dried figs, cut in eighths
2 cans (4-ounce size) blanched whole almonds
2 cans (4½-ounce size) flaked coconut
1 can (8-ounce size) pecan halves
1 jar (4-ounce size) diced candied citron
1 jar (4-ounce size) diced candied orange peel
½ cup sherry

Cake Batter
½ cup butter or margarine, softened
2 cups sugar
6 eggs
2 cups unsifted all-purpose flour
¼ cup orange juice

⅓ cup sherry
Fruitcake glaze (see p. 78)
Raisins
Dried apricot halves
Blanched almonds

1. Prepare fruit mixture: In large kettle, combine currants, raisins, figs, almonds, coconut, pecans, citron, orange peel, and ½ cup sherry; using hands, mix well. Let stand at room temperature, covered, overnight.

2. Next day, line a 10-inch tube pan: On heavy brown paper, draw a 16½-inch circle, and cut out. Set pan in center of circle; draw around base of pan and tube. With pencil lines outside, fold paper into eighths; snip off tip. Unfold circle; cut along folds to circle drawn around base of pan. Grease both tube pan and paper well. Fit paper, greased side up, into pan.

3. Make cake batter: Preheat oven to 275°F.

4. In large bowl, with electric mixer at high speed, beat butter, sugar, and 1 egg until smooth and fluffy. Add remaining eggs, one at a time, beating after each addition until light and fluffy.

5. At low speed, beat in flour (in fourths) alternately with orange juice (in thirds), beginning and ending with flour.

6. Add batter to fruit mixture; with hands, mix until well combined. Turn into prepared pan, packing lightly.

7. Bake about 3½ hours, or until cake tester inserted in center comes out clean. Let cool completely in pan on wire rack. Turn out of pan; peel off paper.

8. Wrap cooled cake in cheesecloth that has been soaked in ⅓ cup sherry. Then wrap very tightly in plastic film or foil. Store in refrigerator or in an airtight container. Resoak cheesecloth with sherry as it dries out—about once a week. Store cake 5 to 6 weeks to develop flavor.

9. To serve: Brush cake with fruitcake glaze. Then decorate with raisins, apricot halves, and blanched almonds.

Makes one 6½-pound tube cake.

Fruitcake Glaze

⅓ cup light corn syrup 1 tablespoon water
1 tablespoon lemon juice

1. In small saucepan, combine corn syrup, lemon juice, and water.

2. Bring to boiling; reduce heat, and simmer, stirring, 5 minutes, or until mixture is reduced to ⅓ cup. Let cool completely.

Almond-Ring Cake

9 cans (8-ounce size)   **White Icing**
  almond paste   1 egg white
3½ cups granulated sugar   1 cup confectioners' sugar
9 egg whites (about   ½ teaspoon white vinegar
  1¼ cups)
                                 ¼ cup granulated sugar
Confectioners' sugar

1. In large, heavy saucepan or Dutch oven, combine almond paste, 3½ cups granulated sugar, and 9 egg whites.
2. Heat, over low heat, stirring constantly with a wooden spoon, until mixture feels warm and is smooth. Remove from heat; let cool about 10 minutes.
3. Grease and flour 3 or 4 large cookie sheets.
4. Turn almond mixture onto board lightly sprinkled with confectioners' sugar. Knead a few minutes—until smooth. Set aside 1 cup of dough for decoration.
5. Preheat oven to 325°F.
6. Keeping hands and work surface coated with confectioners' sugar, shape some of dough into a ½- to ¾-inch-thick rope 5 inches long. Make 16 or 17 more ropes, each 1¼ inches longer than the preceding rope. Shape each into a ring, pinching ends together.
7. Place on cookie sheets, allowing 2 inches between each. With thumb and forefinger, pinch each ring all around so that rings will be broad at base and come to a sharp crease on top.
8. Bake 15 to 20 minutes, or until light golden. Place cookie sheets on wire racks; cool 15 minutes. With spatula, loosen rings carefully, and remove to wire racks; let cool completely.
9. Divide reserved dough into 10 pieces. Roll 8 pieces into 14-inch-long strips. Shape each on cookie sheets into S, for side of cake. Cut remaining 2 pieces in half; roll each into 8-inch strip. Shape on cookie sheet into P for top of cake. Bake about 10 minutes.
10. Make white icing: Place egg white, confectioners' sugar, and vinegar in small bowl. With electric mixer at medium speed, beat until soft peaks form when beater is slowly raised. Place in pastry bag with writing tip.
11. To assemble cake: Place largest ring on a napkin (to keep it from sliding) on a large cake plate. Pipe icing in zigzag fashion on ring. Repeat with remaining rings, stacking in decreasing size and icing, ending with

smallest ring. Also pipe icing on both sides of decorations. This can be done a few days ahead. When icing is completely dry, wrap cake and decorations tightly with plastic film.

12. On the day of serving, melt granulated sugar in small frying pan; heat until golden. Dip S shapes in melted sugar, and "glue" them on cake. For top: Dip bottoms of P shapes in melted sugar; "glue" to top ring, standing up all around so that loops meet in center. If desired, insert a small Danish and a small American flag in top ring.

13. To serve: Lift off rings as needed and break into 2- to 3-inch pieces. Makes 25 to 30 servings.

COOKIES

Honey Cookies

1⅓ cups honey	2 tablespoons finely chopped
1 cup dark-brown sugar,	preserved ginger
firmly packed	1 egg
1 cup butter or margarine	6 cups unsifted all-
1 tablespoon cinnamon	purpose flour
2 teaspoons baking soda	
1½ teaspoons ground cloves	**Frosting**
¼ cup finely chopped	2 egg whites
blanched almonds	2 cups confectioners' sugar
2 tablespoons finely	1 teaspoon white vinegar
chopped candied citron	Red, green, and yellow
	food coloring

1. In large saucepan, combine honey, brown sugar, and butter. Cook over medium heat, stirring occasionally, until butter is melted and mixture comes to boiling. Pour into a large bowl; cool, stirring occasionally, until mixture is lukewarm—about 45 minutes.

2. With wooden spoon, stir in cinnamon, soda, and cloves. Then stir in almonds, citron, ginger, and the egg until well blended. Gradually stir in flour until well combined—dough will be very stiff.

3. Refrigerate the dough, covered, overnight, or for as long as a week.

4. Preheat oven to 375°F. Lightly grease cookie sheets.

5. Remove one-quarter of dough from refrigerator, and roll out on lightly floured surface to a 10-inch square about ¼ inch thick.

6. With 2- or 3-inch cookie cutters, cut into desired shapes. With spatula, place, 1 inch apart, on prepared cookie sheet. Reroll trimmings, and cut out.

7. Bake 8 to 10 minutes, or until cookies are lightly browned. Then remove cookies to wire rack; let cool completely.

8. Repeat with remaining dough.

9. Make frosting: In medium bowl, with electric mixer at medium speed, beat egg whites with sugar and vinegar until thick and soft peaks form when beater is slowly raised.

10. Remove three-fourths of icing, and divide into 3 small bowls. Tint icing in one bowl red; second bowl, green; and third bowl, yellow.

11. Decorate cookies using tinted and white frostings in pastry bags with a writing tip. Or use 4 paper cones: For each, roll 8-inch square of paper on diagonal to form a point. Tape together to secure. Cut off tip of cone to make a $\frac{1}{10}$-inch opening.

12. To store cookies: When frosting is dry, store in a plastic container with tight-fitting lid or in a cookie jar. Place a piece of bread or apple with cookies. Cookies will soften. Store at least 2 weeks to mellow.

Makes 10 to 11 dozen.

Swedish Ginger Cookies

⅓ cup light-brown sugar, firmly packed	1½ teaspoons baking soda
⅓ cup light molasses	⅓ cup butter or margarine
½ teaspoon ground ginger	1 egg
½ teaspoon cinnamon	2½ cups sifted all-purpose flour
½ teaspoon ground allspice	
½ teaspoon ground cloves	Snow frosting (see p. 82)

1. In medium saucepan, combine sugar, molasses, ginger, cinnamon, allspice, and cloves. Cook over medium heat, stirring occasionally, till mixture comes to boiling. Remove from heat.

2. Stir in soda (mixture will bubble up). Then stir in butter until melted.

3. With electric mixer or rotary beater, beat in egg until thoroughly blended.

4. With mixer at low speed or with wooden spoon, gradually beat in 2 cups of the flour to make a stiff dough.

5. Sprinkle remaining flour on board. Turn out dough; knead until all flour is taken up and dough is smooth.

6. Shape into a ball; wrap in waxed paper or plastic film. Refrigerate overnight. (Dough may be stored several days.)

7. Next day: Preheat oven to 350°F. Lightly grease cookie sheets. Divide dough into fourths.

8. On lightly floured surface, roll out one-fourth of dough as thin as possible—less than ⅛ inch thick. Cut out with assorted cookie cutters. Place cookies on prepared cookie sheets.

9. Bake 6 to 8 minutes, or until lightly brown. Remove to wire rack; cool completely.

10. Make snow frosting (you will need 2 batches). Using pastry bag with writing tip, decorate cookies.

11. Store cookies in an airtight container.

Makes about 8 dozen medium-sized cookies.

Snow Frosting

2 egg whites	⅛ teaspoon cream of tartar
2 cups confectioners' sugar	

In medium bowl, with electric mixer at medium speed, beat egg whites with sugar and cream of tartar until mixture is thick and stiff peaks form when beater is raised.

Makes about 1 cup.

Note: Make and use 1 batch at a time.

Finnish Logs

¾ cup butter or margarine	1 egg, slightly beaten
1 teaspoon almond extract	¼ cup finely chopped
⅓ cup sugar	blanched almonds
2 cups sifted all-	1½ teaspoons sugar
purpose flour	

1. Preheat oven to 350°F. and grease 2 cookie sheets.

2. Work butter or margarine with almond extract until soft. Gradually add sugar, and continue working until mixture is creamy.

3. Stir in flour thoroughly, using your hands to make the dough hold together. Pinch off one-fifth of dough, and shape into a roll (use the palm of your hand) about 12 inches long and as thick as your finger. Make 5 of these long thin rolls, and put them side by side on breadboard.

4. With one cut of the knife, slice all 5 rolls at once into 2-inch-long sections. Brush surface of cookies with egg, and sprinkle with a mixture of almonds and sugar.

5. Place 2 inches apart on cookie sheets; bake 15 minutes, or until delicately browned.

Makes 35.

Almond Lace Wafers

¾ cup grated unblanched almonds	1 tablespoon unsifted all-purpose flour
½ cup butter or margarine	1 tablespoon heavy cream
½ cup sugar	1 tablespoon milk

1. Preheat oven to 350°F. Grease 2 cookie sheets generously and coat with flour.

2. Work almonds through a nut grater, or blend in an electric blender until mealy. (Don't grind them through a food grinder—the nuts get too oily.) Measure correct amount.

3. Mix nuts and all remaining ingredients in a saucepan. Cook over low heat, stirring constantly, until butter or margarine melts.

4. Drop teaspoonfuls of the mixture on cookie sheet, just 5 or 6 at a time; bake 8 to 9 minutes, or until cookies turn a light caramel color, with the centers still bubbling.

5. Let cool 1 minute; then transfer, top side down, to paper towels. Roll immediately over the handle of a wooden spoon.

6. Regrease and reflour cookie sheet before baking each batch.

Makes about 2 dozen.

Upsala Holiday Cookies

½ cup butter or margarine, softened	3 tablespoons finely chopped blanched almonds
6 tablespoons sugar	1½ tablespoons sugar
1 tablespoon sherry	1 egg yolk
1½ cups unsifted all-purpose flour	1 teaspoon water

1. In medium bowl, with electric mixer at medium speed, beat butter with 6 tablespoons sugar until light and fluffy. Beat in sherry.

2. With wooden spoon, stir in flour until well blended.

3. Refrigerate, covered, 30 minutes.
4. Preheat oven to 375°F.
5. On lightly floured surface, roll out dough, one half at a time, to ¼-inch thickness. Cut with 1½-inch round cookie cutter. Place, 1 inch apart, on ungreased cookie sheets.
6. Mix almonds with 1½ tablespoons sugar. Beat egg yolk with 1 teaspoon water; brush lightly on cookies. Sprinkle with almond mixture.
7. Bake 15 to 20 minutes, or until lightly browned. Remove to wire rack; let cool completely.
8. Store in tightly covered container in a cool, dry place. (Will keep several weeks.)

Makes about 3 dozen.

Danish Spice Cookies

3½ cups sifted cake flour	1 teaspoon baking soda
1 teaspoon cinnamon	1 tablespoon boiling water
½ teaspoon ground allspice	½ cup finely chopped
½ teaspoon ground cloves	blanched almonds
½ teaspoon ground cardamom	1 teaspoon grated orange peel
¾ cup butter or margarine	
½ cup light-brown sugar, firmly packed	Blanched almonds or candied cherries, for decoration
½ cup dark corn syrup	

1. Sift flour with cinnamon, allspice, cloves, and cardamom. Set aside.
2. In medium saucepan, combine butter, sugar, and corn syrup; cook over medium heat, stirring constantly, until sugar is melted and mixture is hot, but not boiling. Remove from heat.
3. Dissolve soda in boiling water; stir into hot mixture. Pour into large bowl; let cool to lukewarm.
4. Stir in chopped almonds and orange peel. Add flour mixture, half at a time, stirring after each addition until well blended.
5. Refrigerate, covered, overnight.
6. Next day, preheat oven to 375°F. Lightly grease cookie sheets. Divide dough in fourths.
7. On lightly floured surface, roll out one-fourth of dough to about a ten-inch square—dough will be thin. Cut with 3½-inch diamond, or 2½-inch round, fluted cookie cutter. Reroll scraps, and cut. Place on prepared cookie sheets. Decorate each with almond half or candied cherry. Repeat with rest of dough.

8. Bake 6 to 8 minutes, or until lightly browned. Remove to wire rack; cool completely.

9. Store cookies in an airtight container.

Makes about 8 dozen.

Lemon Swedish Cookies

½ cup butter or margarine,
  softened
1 cup unsifted all-
  purpose flour
¼ cup sugar
1 egg yolk
2 tablespoons ground
  blanched almonds
½ teaspoon almond extract

Lemon Filling
1 egg
1 egg yolk
½ cup sugar
¼ cup butter or margarine
1 tablespoon grated lemon peel
¼ cup lemon juice

1. Preheat oven to 400°F.

2. In medium bowl, with pastry blender, cut ½ cup soft butter into the flour and ¼ cup sugar until mixture resembles coarse crumbs.

3. Add 1 egg yolk, the almonds, and almond extract; stir with fork until well blended. Press tablespoonful of mixture into each of eighteen 2-inch fluted tart pans.

4. Bake 10 to 12 minutes, or until golden. Remove to wire rack. Let cool about 5 minutes. Loosen around side with small spatula, and turn out of pans. Let cool on wire rack.

5. Meanwhile, make lemon filling: In top of double boiler, combine egg and egg yolk; beat with spoon just until blended. Add sugar, butter, lemon peel, and lemon juice.

6. Cook over hot, not boiling, water, stirring constantly, until consistency of mayonnaise—about 10 minutes. Turn into small bowl; place waxed paper directly on surface. Refrigerate until well chilled.

7. Just before serving, fill each tart shell with 2 teaspoonfuls of lemon filling.

Makes 1½ dozen.

Old-Fashioned Gingerbread

2½ cups sifted all-
  purpose flour
1 teaspoon baking powder
¾ teaspoon baking soda

1 teaspoon ground ginger
2 teaspoons ground
  cinnamon
½ teaspoon ground cloves

1 teaspoon salt	2 eggs
½ cup butter or margarine, softened	1 cup dark molasses
½ cup sugar	1 cup hot water

1. Preheat oven to 350°F. Lightly grease a 9-by-9-by-1¾-inch baking pan. Line bottom with waxed paper; grease paper lightly.
2. Sift flour with baking powder, soda, spices, salt; set aside.
3. In large bowl of electric mixer, at medium speed, cream butter with sugar until light and fluffy.
4. Add eggs; beat till very light.
5. Mix molasses with hot water.
6. At low speed, beat in flour mixture (in 3 additions) alternately with molasses and water (in 2 additions), beginning and ending with flour mixture. Beat just until smooth; do not overbeat.
7. Turn batter into prepared pan, spreading evenly. Bake 40 to 45 minutes, or until cake tester inserted in center comes out clean.
8. Let cool in pan, on wire rack, for 5 minutes. Gently turn out.
9. Serve warm, with one of toppings (see below). Or cool; frost with frosting (see next page), or top with confectioners' sugar.
Makes 9 servings.

Gingerbread Cupcakes

1. Preheat oven to 350°F. Grease and flour the bottoms of twenty 2½-inch cupcake cups.
2. Make old-fashioned gingerbread batter (see above), using 3 cups flour. Spoon into cupcake cups; fill two-thirds full. Bake about 20 minutes, or till surface springs back when gently pressed with fingertip.
3. Let cool 2 or 3 minutes; then remove from pan. Serve warm, with one of toppings (see below).
Makes 20 2½-inch cupcakes.

TOPPINGS AND FROSTING FOR GINGERBREAD

Apricot Cream Topping

1 teaspoon lemon juice	¼ cup sugar
½ cup apricot nectar	Dash salt
¼ cup dried apricots, finely chopped	3 egg yolks, beaten
	½ cup heavy cream

1. In medium saucepan, combine lemon juice, apricot nectar, apricots, sugar, and salt; bring to boiling, stirring. Reduce heat; simmer, uncovered, 5 minutes.

2. Add some of hot mixture to egg yolks; mix well. Return to saucepan. Cook, stirring, over low heat, until mixture thickens and mounds— about 5 minutes.

3. Remove from heat; cool completely. Whip cream just until stiff. Fold into cooled apricot mixture. Refrigerate, covered.

4. To serve, spoon over warm gingerbread.
Makes 1½ cups.

Lemon Topping

1 package (3⅝-ounce size)   2 cups light cream
   instant lemon-pudding mix

1. With rotary beater, beat pudding with light cream until well blended —about 1 minute. Refrigerate 10 minutes, or until serving.

2. Just before serving, beat until fluffy.
Makes about 2⅓ cups.

Honey Cream Topping

1 cup heavy cream   ¼ cup honey
¼ teaspoon nutmeg

1. In small bowl, beat heavy cream with nutmeg until thick.

2. Gradually add honey, beating constantly. Continue beating until soft peaks form when beater is raised.
Makes about 2 cups.

Lemon-Cream-Cheese Frosting

1 package (3-ounce size)   ¼ cup finely chopped walnuts
   cream cheese, softened   2 tablespoons seedless raisins,
1 tablespoon lemon juice   finely chopped
2 teaspoons grated lemon peel
2¼ cups sifted
   confectioners' sugar

1. In small bowl, with portable electric mixer, beat cheese, lemon juice, lemon peel until fluffy.

2. Gradually add sugar, beating until smooth. Stir in walnuts and raisins. Use to frost top of cooled gingerbread.
Makes about 1 cup.

Index